But Pain Crept In

Shelaine Strom

In the Midst Publishing

For my community

Acknowledgements

This is God's story that I have the privilege of telling. This book's writing is also due to our community of family and friends who faithfully walked with us, and continue to do so. Thank you.

Along the way I treasured the eagle eyes, and thoughtful minds, of reviewers, including:

Rosabelle Birch, Karen Stobbe, Loranne Brown, Riley Strom, Helen Konrad, Virginia Strom, Priscilla Strom, and Paula Thiessen.

A special thanks to Sue Braid for her reviews, and the idea and effort to shape the study questions at the end of the book.

Wendy Toews—your initiatives on our behalf reduced our stress and left us feeling loved beyond measure.

And thank you to family and friends for allowing me to share part of your story as it intertwines with mine.

This medical story would have a much different ending without the support and skill of my family doctor, Kenneth Ng, and my surgeon, David Psutka. I am grateful.

And always, I couldn't write without the unwavering support and belief in me that my husband, Bill, freely provides. I love you!

But Pain Crept In

Prologue

The faces looming over me are familiar, each with a knotted expression. Their lips are moving but they appear mute. Blackness. My eyelids press hard against the weight of unconsciousness. I am shaded from the shocking blue Arizona sky by the circle of tall bodies towering above. *Where am I?*

My left hand can't clench. It just sweats in my baseball glove, limp by my side. My right hand claws at hot sand, grasping, dropping. I am on the ground. But where? The answer must be beyond the shins surrounding me. I turn my head. *Aaahh.* Searing hot jolts fire up my jawline, bursting through the joints, igniting my temples. I can only hear pain. *Talk louder, people. Tell me how this happened!*

No, don't move me! My head will disintegrate. My mouth won't cooperate and let me scream. *No, I can't sit up.* They need to stop sliding their hands under my shoulders and pushing me up. I'm spinning. I can't see. Blackness. "Hold her head," I hear up close in the distance. Someone is behind me, supporting me. Another dabbing at my lip. Blood.

I am on the pitcher's mound, home plate warping in and out of focus. The pitcher's mound. We were told to run out to the field for catching practice. Coach would hit fly balls and we'd improve our fielding game. I grabbed my glove and shoved it on as I jogged toward second base. "Shelaine," I heard yelled from home plate, along with the familiar crack of ball meeting bat. I threw my momentum over my left shoulder and turned back to answer the call. The line-drive had my name on it.

The strike on my left chin spun my head viciously right. Muscles, tendons and bones flew into action, preventing my head from completing the wild trajectory. Simultaneously, my sloshing brain slammed into skull plates, dropping me to the dirt unconscious; the velocity of impact fracturing my mandible ear to ear, punching condyle heads through cartilage, smashing bones against zygomatic arches. This is no ordinary broken jaw.

Stop moving me. I'm going to be sick. They can't hear me. My bloodied lips won't part, my tongue races around, counting teeth, checking for absences. All present but relocated. The molars don't meet. Only my top eye teeth touch my lower front teeth. Something's not right. "Sit here on the bench. Would you like some water?" *I would. I'm parched.* The cup is rattling in my hand and I can't still it. "Here Zed, let me help you." Zed. Only one friend calls me that because I'm a Canadian transplant to Mesa. Her alphabet ends in zee, mine with zed. Ninth grade girls have a way with nicknames.

"Okay, girls, back to the field." I can't move. He can't mean me. No, I'm staying here for now, at least until I'm sure I won't throw up. The field is swirling, pulsing in unison with the waves of pain that shoot chin to forehead. The bleeding has stopped but I feel my face expanding. I want to get out of here. I'm tired. Maybe I could lie down. This dugout bench is too narrow, so hard. I should go home.

They are back around me again. Someone said practice is over, that it's time to go. I'm walking across the school-yard, heading toward my house, I think. Each teammate peels off as we pass the school front and I'm alone. I don't know if I have my bag or glove, I just take a next step. My feet seem to know the route without my help. Enrose Street, Evergreen Street, Elmwood Street, Encanto Street. Turn right. More steps to the side door. No one will be home at this time of day.

* * *

It's been two days since the knockout. I'm sitting on an examination table while a doctor mumbles "left cheek hematoma, cellulitis, antibiotics, come back next week, no further tests." Go home and wait for this one event to impact the rest of your life.

* * *

I should be able to open my mouth by now, it's been 5 weeks. The dental surgeon is concerned and fears the punctured cartilage has formed scar tissue, like a donut. When the condyle head wants to move forward it bumps into the evidence of trauma and sends fiery signals that motion is restricted. Dr. Borgesen is prescribing a bite splint to see if holding my teeth apart by a quarter of an inch will let the joint rest and heal. I think it's too late.

February 21, 1980 marks the first day the hard acrylic plate snapped on my upper teeth. It is annoying and makes my challenged speech more so. I struggle to open wide enough to clasp it into place. It's cumbersome and awkward, not something a 14-year-old longs to sport. But all is not lost. I've recently been introduced to Jolly Rancher green apple candies. School rules prevent us from eating during class but who would know if the girl with the broken face and mumbled words had one stuck to her appliance? Rebel.

* * *

The plate isn't working. I have less than a half-inch opening and pain is escalating. I can't bite, chew or think straight. Percodan is my new best friend. Dr. Borgesen says I'm too young to be on so many medications. Something must be done. But I'm so young. Only 15. He's never operated on anyone my age. He wants another opinion, one that matters to him. He wants to know how Dr. Morgan, the inventor of the procedure he's considering performing on me, sees the situation. A speed trip to Los Angeles on August 4, 1980 and the plan is confirmed.

It will require four incisions, two in front of my ears and two on my neck. He assures me that the scars won't be noticeable when they have healed. Yes, there have to be four cuts so a wire can be inserted from the lower openings to hook on the bone and dislocate the jaw. Then he will take the damaged cartilage out of each side and line the joints with the metal. At least, that is how I understand it.

Everything in this room is stainless steel except me, and soon that will change. August 7th—the day my jaw joints will be lined with cutting-edge 1980 technology—the Morgan Prosthesis. The thin, molded metal plates—are they stainless steel? I can't remember—will replace my punctured, scarred, donut-ring cartilage when the bilateral temporomandibular arthroplasty is complete. I'll have two screws on each cheekbone holding the units in place and in just over four hours, I will make history for my surgeon. I never wanted to be this kind of famous.

It's so quiet in here, and cold. The nurse rolled me in here alone, left without a word or even a blanket. This sheet is too thin. My body is trembling from the inside out. I hope someone comes soon. Only this light of seven eyes above is keeping watch over me.

* * *

A success. I hear them talking about me but they don't know it. Too much work to open my eyes. Something is squeezing my head. Bandages. A curly-cue on top of my head. My mom's voice. Others' too. Let me sleep.

Help! I can't breathe! It's dark. Where am I? Someone's choking me. Who has their hands around my throat? A button, push the panic button. No, I can't hold still, I can't breathe! A snip. Another. It's like being so far under water. I'm pulling hard to the surface. I can see the light above. *I want air! Pull harder!* The scissors snip another layer of white gauze open! I'm almost there. Finally, that life-giving gasp and oxygen saturates my starving lungs. *Yes, that's better.* Yes, the bandages were the problem—too tight with all the swelling. *Thank you. Thank you.* Sleep now.

"Don't worry, everything will be okay." The nurse looks worried. There's an alarm going off. The hospital is on fire, I hear someone say. Our wing doesn't have to be evacuated. It's in the kitchen. I don't care. I must sleep.

I can go home now, four days later, bruised and fat-faced, but able to open wide for the first time in eight months, and for the next 31 years.

PART I

The Backdrop

For over three decades life progressed with little attention to bones rubbing on metal. I graduated from Trinity Western University in Langley, British Columbia with a degree in Social Sciences and a hope to affect change in the lives of people. The first stop on my career path kept me at the university, working as an assistant to the Director of Community Life and positioning me in that "new staff" orientation group with a recent addition to the faculty. While I don't remember meeting him that day, Bill will tell you that we shared get to know you activities. He followed up on that a few days later when, at a chance encounter, he said, "Hey, we've both been to Hong Kong. We should get together for coffee some time and exchange stories." Cheesy line perhaps, but it worked. August 6, 1988, one year later, we were married.

During that time I began experiencing discomfort in my jaw joints and ended up in a specialist's office in Vancouver where I met Dr. Epstein for the first set of visits before a thirty-year gap. He hadn't heard of my particular implants but diagnosed inflammation in the surrounding tissues and injected cortisone into the joints, a treatment that gave me relief for years.

Married and eager to begin my professional career, I entered the realm of social work boldly in a position that challenged me at every turn.

"Shelaine Strom, pursuant to Section 3(4) of the Family and Child Service Act, I do hereby delegate to you, an employee of the Ministry of Social Services and Housing, the powers, duties, functions and capabilities of the Act..." With that official proclamation, the Deputy Superintendent of Family and Child Services deemed me qualified to investigate allegations of abuse and neglect and intervene in ways that could change families forever. What were they thinking?

It was January of 1989 and at age 23 "social worker" became my first post-university title. I covered vacancies in various offices as an auxiliary float and received immersion training in family caseload management, intake and conducting investigations. My co-workers commented on my quick and organized approach to assignments and my 700-hour appraisal noted my "very calm exterior even in very tense circumstances." I took that as affirmation and promptly ignored the remainder of the paragraph: "...this may lead her supervisors to assume that the lack of outward nervousness indicates a lack of need for direction." The evaluation went on to encourage me to "take responsibility for ensuring that all my questions are answered and my need for direction and consultation are met." Propped by my need to perform and look professional, I focused on the self-sufficient persona and swallowed my stress as I acted the role.

A colleague's maternity leave gave me long-term placement and my own caseload that summer. I fit in with the staff and took up my share of duties including a weekly shift on intake. These became a day of prayer for silent phones as any call would potentially require me to set aside all current work and maintain my calm exterior in potentially very tense circumstances.

But the phone did ring.

"Hello, my name is Anne and I am a public health nurse. I received a report from the manager of a local motel that he is worried about one of his long-term residents. She appears to be pregnant and he observes her chain smoking, drinking vodka straight from the bottle and he suspects she is using drugs as well, although he could not confirm that. Our records indicate that she is 41 years old, has been diagnosed with schizophrenia and this is her third known pregnancy. We completed an assessment on her and attempted pre-natal care but she has refused all assistance. Her unborn child is at risk now and most certainly once born."

With that conversation, this pregnant woman became my concern. My case. That's what we called these people. Our caseload. I'll call her Shirley to protect her privacy.

Armed with background notes, pen and a foggy recollection of schizophrenia from my abnormal psychology text, I signed out of the office and drove alone to the Shooting Star motel. The neon "manager's office" sign blinked sporadically at the far end of the U-shaped complex. I struggled to locate numbers and parked halfway down the row of the pay-by-the-month accommodations. The door to unit 16 was propped open. I rapped on the frame and announced my name, asking to speak with her. No response and yet I knew people were home. I could hear their conversation. Slightly irritated with being ignored, I knocked louder and repeated my request, including my job title.

With eyes adjusting to the dim, I saw a mound on the living room floor. Baby sleepers, t-shirts, socks, undershirts, dresses, more sleepers, more socks, booties, hats. Hundreds, thousands of items—all pink—in a heap five feet wide and nearing the ceiling.

I made one more appeal for contact, shouting into the voices chattering around the corner and then, silence. Nothing. "May I come in?" I rasped. Calmly and convincingly, she replied, "If you come in my house, I will kill you."

I couldn't hear her next sentence from the safety of my car.

Roughly two months later, the public health nurse called again. My client's case was back on my desk. Shirley had given birth. A boy. Five pounds, four ounces. The next morning, with mental health assessments in hand, I drove to the hospital to deliver news that I would be apprehending her child.

This time I brought a seasoned co-worker and we found Shirley sitting just inside her hospital room, drinking coffee. I crossed in front of her and sat in the only other chair, beyond the bed, by the window. My colleague stood at the door. My client ignored the introductions and I got down to business.

I've often wondered what I expected from her. "Thank you for coming, Shelaine. Of course you are well-meaning and have only the best interest of my child in mind. Yes, I acknowledge that my mental illness prevents me from adequately caring for this boy and yes, I really only wanted a girl. So please, take him and find him a good home." No. She threw her coffee at my head—cup and all—and lunged across the bed with screaming wild eyes. I cannot recall how I got to the corridor. My fellow worker's only words en route to the office were, "Never let the client get between you and your escape route." That I remember.

Two days later I took the baby into the care of the Ministry. I watched as the nurse buckled him into the car seat, paying careful attention so I would be able to get him out at the foster home. With diaper bag slung over my shoulder, I picked up my bundle and feigned confidence as I stepped into the elevator.

Three floors down, I proceeded toward the exit, fully expecting security to arrest me for kidnapping. My poseur-parent guise thinned and began to crumble as the reality that I, Child-Social Worker myself, was for that moment the closest thing this beautiful, innocent little boy had to a parent. I struggled through moist eyes to fasten his seat into the car and sniffled my way across town to his temporary home. No crying he made.

Day after day I spent my lunch break poring over "approved potential parents" from head office. I read story after story of couples pleading their case for why the next infant should become theirs. Some were date stamped more than five years earlier. I strained to breathe. What was I doing? Who was I to pick out the forever-family of this child? What qualified me to play God and determine his future? I tried to rub the weight of responsibility out of my aching neck.

Within three months I passed the little man over to his adoptive parents—dad, a teacher and mom, a psychiatric nurse. My supervisor commended me for the speed of the process.

Months after the apprehension, while on a lunch walk, I heard the voices. Over my shoulder I saw her reflection in a bank of glass behind me on the empty street, gaining ground, spewing expletives, arms flailing. I sprinted back to the office, arriving out of breath. My co-workers mockingly laughed. "She likely didn't even know it was you!" The muscle tension in my whole being told me I had thought otherwise.

*　*　*

I became pregnant in July, 1989 and managed to hide the low-grade morning sickness through the first trimester. By six months I could hardly walk and, with one day's notice, my doctor ordered me off work as my hips screamed for no apparent reason. Perhaps it was a foreshadowing of the whole-body toll the ever-growing misalignment of my jaw would later have.

Our first son, Taylor, born in April, 1990, marked my shift from career track to stay-at-home mom. My husband and I valued my presence with our children and committed to a one-paycheck lifestyle. Within 18 months Clark joined our family and, a short 25 months later, we welcomed Eric. And with that third "It's a boy!" announcement I suspected my future would be active.

And it was. Delightfully so. Limited income dictated frugality so vacationing and camping became our go-to getaway plan. We explored our province's natural beauty with our ten-man, two room tent as home base. In the early days, we cooked all our food over a campfire. At times, I must confess, I did wonder why we called this activity a holiday when caring for three little boys without the modern conveniences of home exponentially increased the workload. The morning baby Clark crawled through the previous night's campfire remnants comes to mind. Cold water does not easily remedy a soot-stained face but the white Chiclets teeth smiling through his chubby blackened cheeks did melt my irritated heart.

Park rangers became our friends providing nighttime campfire stories and guided outings by day. We explored trails and bogs learning rules of the forest and facts about flora and fauna. Clark's Nutcracker became a family favorite in the bird world as we grew together in our appreciation for all the West Coast has to offer, including hikes. With boys as young as three, five and seven we trekked the Lightning Lake Loop at Manning Park and even tackled Frosty Mountain trail, despite its difficult rating.

One summer during this season of adventuring, we accepted an invitation to stay with friends in the Okanagan. The surrounding mountains called us to hike any one of numerous trails that gained elevation and promised intoxicating vistas of lake, mountains and distant city. The boys grew excited at the prospect of sighting Lake Okanagan's Ogopogo, British Columbia's own Loch Ness monster.

"I'm sure Denise said the path broke off this main road up the hill. It should be coming up soon," I assured my family.

"Here's a place we can head up," Bill announced, pointing to slightly trodden foliage off to the right. "If this isn't the main trail it will likely bump into it soon enough." Too bad we hadn't read the local hikes brochure warning us to pay close attention to the red markers and not be led astray by countless animal trails.

The brothers—as they had come to refer to each other—needed no convincing and bounded through the brittle Okanagan summer grass. The thin corridor gained elevation rapidly, something we expected given the description by our friend and host. "It's two or three kilometers up and pretty steep but you guys can do it. It should only take you an hour or so to get to the top and it's so worth it. The view is incredible. Once you've climbed Pincushion Mountain you can say you're a true Peachlander." We were sold.

The trail wound around and up and back and up some more as our fresh legs took us deep onto the mountain face through sagebrush and ponderosa pine. We covered ground quickly, gaining height while navigating the rocky path—all with a growing internal sense that we were not on the main trail.

The path progressively became more broken rock than foot-packed dirt as we passed the one-hour marker. Our oldest son, Taylor, age 8, blazed trail with his brothers Clark, 6½, and Eric, 4, close behind. "Ouch," yelled Eric. "Stop knocking rocks down, Taylor! That one hit me in the head!" Eric's plea caught the attention of Bill and me as we called everyone to a halt and surveyed our surroundings. When did we get onto this enormous shale-like landslide? And more importantly, how were we going to get off it?

"Guys," Bill started, "we're going to have to climb up this rock pile side by side. Every time we step up the rocks are going to fall on the people below." With that, we five became a horizontal line across the face of the loose mountain and slowly picked our way up. We had been warned to watch out for bears and rattlesnakes but no one mentioned falling rocks! Perhaps they'd never taken this route.

Our mountain goat children reveled in the extra adventure as Bill and I pushed to keep up. Clark, on the outer edge of our human chain, announced, "Hey, here's a path!" He scrambled off the shale and took off on yet another not so well traveled track. His brothers followed close behind on the thin alleyway between sheer rock face up and steep cliff down.

Clark led us along the precarious edge, seemingly oblivious to the potential. My heart raced and a sickening sense that we were lost and in danger grew rapidly. I looked back at my husband whose face shared my sentiment. "Clark. Stop. Guys, we need to stop and figure out where we are." The boys ground to a halt before rounding one more curve and sat on a rock ledge to wait for us to join them. Bill stepped past the kids to survey the path ahead. "Ah, Shelaine. There is no path. It drops off right here. It's just a cliff. Guys, we need to pray and ask God for help."

Taylor piped up. "This is just like the tape we were listening to in the van. You know, the song they sang about God commanding his angels to guard you." And so we prayed, asking God to command his angels concerning us to guard us in all our ways; that they would lift us up in their hands and we would not strike our feet against a stone. (Psalm 91:11-12). We parents added a silent prayer of forgiveness for putting our family in danger and asked for God's mercy in spite of our stupidity. He answered.

With "amen" we opened our eyes and looked around. Three sides cliff. But directly above our heads, about three feet up, a path. And not just any bunny trail. The path. The one with two inch by two inch red metal squares of life-giving direction nailed to trees. Within five minutes we reached the summit and drank in the panoramic vista of Okanagan Lake from Kelowna to Penticton and Okanagan Mountain Park across the water. We gathered around the Canadian flag for the family photo op as victorious climbers, reveling in God's protection and creation. Taking the marked trail down felt satisfyingly dull.

That night my family dropped into adventure-exhausted sleep while I struggled to get comfortable. Hips whined, knees ached, and mid-back burned, overpowering my intense fatigue and keeping me awake.

A myriad of tests had been performed the year after Eric's birth with inconclusive results. Fibromyalgia, my doctor had landed on. The diagnosis for the persistent, unexplained muscle pain never felt satisfactory to me but I attended the workshop on how to live well and felt relieved it wasn't something more serious.

And because the Morgan Prosthesis continued to do its job in unprecedented fashion, no one suspected my jaw to be at the root. In fact, most recipients of similar implants experienced such pain and complications that they required removal of the metal within five short years. Eighteen years later my mandibles silently scraped and bumped away on the metal, secretly destroying the joints.

* * *

With elementary school came volunteerism. Taylor entered the small, upstart Christian school located in a collection of mobiles on the campus of a long established high school. At God's prompting, I began a weekly Mom's Who Care prayer group—lovingly called See Who Cares by four-year-old Eric—which eventually birthed a Care Ministry designed to shower our staff with encouragement. The school grew in enrollment, built a new building and the parent organization flourished.

While serving on the Parent Advisory Council (PAC) as Care Ministry Coordinator, I also volunteered as our church's representative on the larger school board. I moved into the PAC president position and, one year later, was elected to the school board executive as Director of Personnel. I held the two positions simultaneously for one year and then carried on with board work for a total of five years.

Bill and I had agreed that finding ministry opportunities we could do separately worked best as we avoided babysitting costs more easily. He served as our church moderator and we planned evening meetings on different nights. We also recognized that my handful of hours per month of paid work was simply not enough to supplement his income and meet the mounting expenses of our growing family. I added more paid work once Eric started school, juggling my roles and coordinating family schedules which now included soccer practices and games, all with one family vehicle.

And I loved it. But by spring of 2005 we were tired and so we coordinated our resignations from all things volunteer and planned our greatest family adventure yet—a month in Indonesia.

Two years prior, long-time friends of ours, Kevin and Allyson Martin, who are missionaries living among a primitive people group in Indonesia, came for a visit and shared stories of jungle adventures. The tales mesmerized. "When can we go and visit them, Mom?" asked our oldest, eyes brimming with thirteen-year-old desire to swing on vines and swim in piranha-infested waters. "Someday," I responded, cringing at the inadequacy of my answer and fully aware the topic was not dead.

Several days later, over dinner, Taylor repeated his question. I suspected that my attempts to put him off further wouldn't satisfy so I began explaining the cost attached to international travel and the current balance in our savings account—zero. Undaunted, he replied, "Well, you guys have always told us that if something is important enough, you make it a priority and work hard to do it. So, if we really want to go to Indonesia, that's what we need to do!"

It quickly became one of those moments where I wished my kids hadn't been listening to what we were teaching them. We knew it was time to practice what we preached.

Several family meetings determined we were all on-board and willing to make the sacrifices required to accomplish such a lofty goal. We discussed how each family member would contribute or give something up. Taylor babysat and had a few odd jobs so he would add a portion of his earnings to the fund. The younger two boys had limited income potential so we brainstormed ideas. Our middle son decided to forego opportunities to snowboard that season and redirected the money to Indonesia travel. The youngest sprang out of his thoughtful silence and offered, "Mom and Dad," he said, "I'm willing to give up having you come and watch some of my soccer games so that you can work more and earn more money!" Bill and I exchanged glances knowing that in Eric's world it was a big sacrifice and he viewed it as an honest contribution to the goal.

Over the next two years we made our trip a priority. It became a go-to point of discerning how we used our time and resources and led to many conversations that sounded a lot like, "How do you think that fits with our plan for Indonesia?" Our kids asked that question of us as often as we posed it to them.

After two years of saving, we spent 34 days traveling, had 17 flights—including helicopter rides in the Balim Valley, akin to zipping through a giant patch of broccoli—and experienced life in the remote jungles of Indonesia. It proved to be a life-changing trip for each of us, particularly in seeing how accomplishing a big dream needs to be achieved in daily decisions.

We returned to Canada healthy and thankful to God for His protection and provisions. The next day Taylor required an emergency appendectomy.

* * *

By fall of 2005 I had lost a few pounds. When weight seemed to fall off disproportionate to food intake and exercise I went for tropical bug testing. No parasites or international freeloaders showed up in my system but the numbers on my scale kept dropping. More tests, specialists and scans were ordered as my energy lagged and I fell below 100 pounds.

In May of 2006 and thirty five pounds lighter, an endocrinologist reviewed my medical history asking, "You've never had a head injury?"

"No," I replied. "I was rear-ended in three separate car accidents within a three-month period at age 18 but that resulted in whiplash and soft tissue damage." Only years later did it occur to me that a broken jaw resulting in loss of consciousness constituted a head injury.

Despite my short sightedness, the specialist diagnosed me with Adrenal Insufficiency—a condition where my body does not produce enough cortisol—and prescribed me a medication that felt like nothing less than a lifesaving intervention. The infusion of cortisol replacement into my depleted system shot instant energy and within days my weight stabilized and began its crawl up from 98 pounds to a healthy level. The medication managed my condition effectively and we found another new normal.

* * *

In the early 90's my career path had shifted from social work to career instruction and coaching when I became connected with Strategic, a company offering workshops to people in job transition. I began as a resource researcher and gradually moved into roles with ever-increasing responsibility, eventually taking on an instructor position and becoming our team's leader. I found my sweet spot.

The company ran a government-funded program called Success@Work and I taught over half the content of the three-week course, sharing new information, facilitating discussion and encouraging frustrated participants in their journey. I gave direction to our small staff and thrived on creating a work environment where both clients and employees felt valued and appreciated. Together our team established a place where people routinely spoke of feeling safe to share their story and supported in their struggles. The position felt made for me.

Many clients came to us feeling broken, beaten down and highly skeptical (that's a kind description for some!). The overtly angry and difficult ones charged my battery as, once won over, they became our most vocal champions. Watching such transformation of attitude and confidence kept me enthusiastically coming back to a new group each month. While we could not speak overtly of God's presence, His Spirit worked through us as we presented our content, like the following session on healthy boundaries.

The projector shone an idyllic scene. A couple canoeing across the calm water of a lake that hugged the base of a snow-capped mountain under bright blue sky, interrupted only by the wisp of cloud circling the mountain peak, filled the background.

"How would you describe this picture?" I asked the group. They responded with "peaceful, serene, gorgeous and tranquil," except one participant who stared skeptically at the screen. "Do you see something different, Tracy?" I inquired.

"Well, it is beautiful, but there's something about that mountain…" Her voice trailed off as she studied the landscape.

"Okay, overall the scene looks quite lovely and inviting but, if we look more closely, perhaps there are clues that all is not as it first seems. It is a mountain, after all. But as you looked at this photo, did you imagine that this was possible?" With that question I advanced the slide showing Mt. St. Helens in full volcanic eruption. The group let out an assortment of chuckles, gasps and "oh wows."

"I think that first picture is like many of us. We do life attempting to look put-together, perhaps even lovely. But internally, we're steaming and, just like the volcano, the pressure inside builds and builds until we can't contain it and then we blow, spewing lava and ash, or in our case, perhaps anger or health issues."

Tracy interjected. "That's totally me. I can go along with things and help people or do stuff for my co-workers and then one day, I lose it. It's like I can't stop myself from being so angry and it just screams out of me. Then I feel like a jerk afterwards because I lose it over really stupid little things."

"So what do you think causes our internal volcanic activity?" I asked the class.

"For me it's when I'm tired," Cam offered. "I'm so much less patient and my fuse is really short."

"I think I get overloaded," Tracy added. "So many people expect so much from me—'Would you help me move? Would you watch my kids? Would you dog-sit for me? Would you take my shift?'—the asking never ends!"

I smiled. "Do you recall our conversation about boundaries? How might angry outbursts and boundaries be connected?"

"Well, I suppose if I'm being honest and saying no, I won't get to feeling overloaded like Tracy said. Then I wouldn't lose my temper as much," Cam conceded.

"That's it," I affirmed. "The first thing to pay attention to is your internal talk. Listen for grumbling and complaining or 'should-ing' all over yourself." I paused as the term sank in and people grinned. "You know, 'I should go, I should say yes, I should help'—that's the language of obligation, not giving freely and if you hear that inside your head, ask yourself what's really going on. Are you talking yourself into a feeling of powerlessness or the 'victim' place? Did you say 'yes' when you really felt 'no'?"

Tracy seemed perplexed again. "That's all great for me to say I have boundary issues, but if I start saying no to people, they are not going to be impressed."

"I agree. You likely will meet some resistance to the changes you make. I think of it in terms of a mobile that hangs over a baby's crib. Each of the little characters dangle and bob evenly, until one day, the baby learns to stand up, grabs on to Tigger and promptly plops down, pulling the tiger completely off the mobile. What happens in that instant when the baby rips Tigger away?"

"Oh, Winnie the Pooh and Eeyore go flying!" shouted Cam.

"Yes, and in those initial moments after the change occurred, chaos appears to have overtaken. But if you endure that wave of bedlam and don't try to rush in to re-attach Tigger, the mobile will eventually settle and find its way to a new place of healthier balance. Relational chaos can take a long time to shift and if we get scared or feel bullied, we may run back and try to re-attach our version of Tigger. The old 'known' can feel more comfortable—even if it's ugly—than the uncertainty of the new 'unknown'."

"So how do I judge if my boundary is a good idea—like say tough love—and when it's just being mean or selfish?" Tracy's face tightened as she anticipated my answer.

"Do you know what one of the key issues is with leprosy?"

"Good grief. Leprosy?" spurted Cam. "What on earth does that have to do with boundaries?"

"I know, it feels like a jump," I conceded and then explained the connection. "Someone with leprosy loses their ability to feel pain. So the disfigurement we associate with the disease is really a result of a person not knowing when his or her body is being injured. For example, someone with leprosy may not know his hand is being burnt before it's severely damaged. The automatic pain reaction to pull away is missing."

"Still lost," said Cam, looking baffled.

"If people don't ever feel the pain attached to their choices and behaviors, they become adult babies, living in a perpetual state of immaturity and not learning what it takes to function in a grown-up world. They may even begin to feel entitled to a free ride because they haven't had to use adult-living muscles. People need to feel the 'hurt' or consequences of their choices to avoid long-term harm to their character."

"But I thought you said we don't set boundaries to change other people. Sounds to me like you're trying to fix them," Tracy challenged.

I chuckled and agreed. "It does, doesn't it? And I'll be the first to admit, this is not an exact science and it's important to have trusted people to talk about these situations with, because we can't always see our way through clearly. That said, when I decide to say no to someone, I'm doing it to protect my wellbeing. It's my *hope* that he will grow from it but that's not my primary *motive*. Does that help?"

Tracy nodded as Cam spoke.

"And how the person takes your boundary says something about them."

"Exactly and it's a good thing for us to ask ourselves, too. How well do we receive boundaries from others? If someone says no to you, do you own that you are sad or mad or do you try to make them bad?"*

---

* Concepts from *Boundaries*, Cloud & Townsend.

Tracy flopped her arms and head on the table with a thump. "Seriously? I can't believe how messed up I am!" She peeked up and added, "From what you say, I have boundary issues everywhere. I can't set them and I can't let others have them either. And, I've blown up like that volcano my whole life. It's really kind of depressing."

I flipped the PowerPoint to the third mountain slide, this one capturing Mt. St. Helens as it appeared a few years post-eruption. "Tracy, it's my understanding that after this mountain exploded, experts claimed that everything covered with lava would be permanently destroyed—that no life would return to the area. You can see that the lake from the first picture is gone and the side of the mountain is replaced with a gaping crater. When we blow up, some things are scarred or changed irreversibly. But that's not the whole story. Look at the landscape. There are flowers growing and small trees and shrubs are returning. Would you agree that this is also a beautiful scene? It's just scenic in a different way."

"Those things didn't grow back overnight, though," Cam said. He told us about his recent visit to the mountain and how, after almost 30 years, the growth is still minimal.

"It's true. New growth takes time. I recall reading about this volcanic area and its recovery and love the phrase scientists use to describe seeds that survived the blast and made that comeback—'resilient restarters.' It's my hope that what we're covering in this program can assist you in building resilience as you re-start your career."

A volcano erupts when the shell of a mountain can no longer contain the pressure of rising magma and gases, sometimes initiated by shifting tectonic plates. Similarly, a jaw explodes unexpectedly when years of bone grinding on metal alter joint physiology, moving implants out of alignment. Both result in chaos, destruction, pain and years of rebuilding. Both require resilient restarters.

*　*　*

"Are we there yet?"

I looked over my shoulder from the passenger seat into the face of our 17-year-old son Eric, his eyes twinkling mischievously. "What do you think?" I poked back, wondering how long this game from his childhood would continue.

"How long is this road? It's taking forever. Dad, didn't you say it was only 12.8 miles from the pavement to the trailhead?"

Bill and I smiled, thankful for Eric's enthusiasm to hike with us even though his two older brothers were working at camp for the summer. Bill braked and carefully steered the van around another pothole. "Can't go any faster on this gravel." More washboard punctuated Bill's statement. He eased off the gas as the van skittered across the corrugated ground and wound into the hairpin curve.

"I'm happy to take our time," I added, pointing out the window, "when that's the alternative." Eric pressed his nose to the window, taking in the fullness of the unguarded road carved tenuously on the edge of a 1000-foot drop.

"Yeah, we would have a long way to fall, wouldn't we? But I think all those trees would stop us before we went all the way down." Eric's eyes glinted with playfulness.

"I'd prefer adventure on the trail, thank you." I reached back and squeezed his knee.

Eric smiled. "Is this the same trail we did with the brothers and Buddy?"

Ah yes, this alpine area had provided countless memories for our family. Just 90 minutes south of our British Columbia home in northwest Washington, Mt. Baker had long been a favorite hiking destination. The snow-capped volcano and its surrounding peaks crawl with trails for all abilities. When the boys were little we'd pick the less strenuous ones, primarily so Bill and I could keep up with their young legs racing along the path.

An early favorite, Ptarmigan Ridge, presented a mostly flat path etched onto the side of the mountain with a survivable gentle slope down, something I'd noted in case one of my little men took a tumble. About halfway to the destination point a unique rock outcropping we called God's amphitheatre provided a natural place to drink our water and munch on granola bars. The rocky terrace begged nimble legs to climb up and over it while Bill and I rested and breathed in peaks, lakes, snow, lupines, asters and daisies.

On Father's Day in 1999, my husband and a team of six others summited Mt. Baker. They hiked into base camp where they pitched tents and attempted to sleep, knowing that their ascent would need to begin by 3:00 a.m. in order to make it to the top and safely down again by dark. They achieved their goal and Bill came home full of stories that captivated our sons' attention. They wanted to go, too.

The next summer we agreed that base camp would be a realistic goal for our then 7-, 9- and 10-year-olds. "Can we bring Buddy? Please?" Our eight pound Multipoo was a good sport but this 5.5 mile hike gaining 1400 feet seemed like a stretch. The boys persisted and we relented. Poor dog.

Buddy never did like traveling in a vehicle and that day proved no different. He whined and yowled over each mile taking consolation from no one. When we arrived at the Heliotrope Ridge trailhead he hit the ground running and we took turns having him "pull" us up the incline. His enthusiasm was contagious and we bounded upwards, until we hit snow, at which point "princess dog" took over.

He gingerly put one paw down, pulled back, shook the foot and shot me the "there is no way I am doing this" look. I pulled on his leash, gently dragging him onto the snow. He held his ground as his butt slid across the frosty patch. Seemingly unimpressed with the chilly ride, he gave in and painstakingly picked his way over the snowy patches. By the time we reached our destination he had snowballs packed to his armpits. I'm not sure Buddy appreciated the view at 5100 feet. We took turns carrying him down the mountain.

"Mom?" Eric brought me back to the present. "Do you remember how quiet Buddy was after that hike? He totally passed out on the floor and didn't move until we got home."

"Yes, poor dog. And that was a different trail. The one we're doing today is called Skyline Divide. Your dad has hiked this one with some guys from work and I've done it with Joey but we haven't been here as a family. And look at that, the parking lot!"

Eric shot out of the van and did his characteristic run of excitement around the trailhead lot. It was worth being enthusiastic. The day had broken as forecast— unlimited visibility, an anticipated high of 22 degrees Celcius—perfect conditions for a mountain adventure.

A quick stretch and bathroom stop. Boots tightened. Sun-screen on. Packs filled with ample water, snacks and appropriate survival gear slung over shoulders. Straps buckled, adjusted and cinched at chest and waist. "Are you ready, Mom?" asked Eric, bouncing with energy and anticipation.

Almost. I reached into the back of the van and pulled out my old ski poles. Recently a chiropractor encouraged me to use hiking poles as a protection for my knees and an aid to hips that periodically balked at my love of climbs and declines. She had given me a thirty-second lesson on how to use them several weeks prior.

We began our ascent of the nine-mile trail in the shaded cool of western hemlock, mountain hemlock and silver fir forest. Within a few hundred feet we encountered the first of many 2½–3 foot tall rock walls. I strained my 5'4" frame up onto the ledge as my six-foot, long-legged partners bounded up effortlessly. After several similar demands I jested, "Hey, check out the length of these legs!" The guys slowed and took turns offering hand-pulls up the taller steps.

For shorter terraces I reached the poles forward and up, planted them on the flat, and hoisted myself to the next level demanding my upper body, not my legs, do the work. Plant, pull, step, repeat—thousands of times. We gained 1500 feet in the first two miles.

"This is amazing!" declared Eric as we broke out of forest to see the exposed mountainside we were about to ascend. The barren slope was highlighted by the trail cutting back and forth repeatedly, winding to the top. Eric broke into a jog as I inhaled deeply and pushed my pace to not be a drag. At one point Eric noticed I had stopped and yelled back, "Do you need to rest, Mom?"

"No," I replied, "I'm just enjoying the view! The trees are lovely." He laughed and resumed his pace.

As expected, Eric reached the ridge, our summit, before us. For the first time since we left the van he stood completely still. Eventually Bill and I joined him in his silence. Six thousand feet above sea level, the sprawling ridge offered unhindered views of Mt. Kulshan to the south, Shuksan to the east and High Divide to the north. There was nothing to say for a long time.

"Let's find a place to have our lunch," Bill suggested. We scouted the area for a patch of ground to rest on, being careful not to destroy any of the surrounding fireweed, valerian, or oxeye daisies. "Remember," Eric noted with a twinkle, "don't damage the flora or fauna." Those countless evening forest ranger shows in campgrounds had taught our boys well.

Our packed lunch satisfied our ravenous appetites while the beauty fed our spirits. We wandered around independently trying to burn the splendour into our minds. I stretched my shoulders back repeatedly trying to work out the ache building through my neck and mid-back. *I am going to be stiff tomorrow.*

I met up with Bill and Eric at a long patch of snow descending down a gentle slope, just begging a youth to slide. I grabbed a handful of God's icepack and applied it to my neck while Eric enjoyed a couple of chilly descents and photo ops. We posed for more pictures and reluctantly agreed it was time to begin our trek down.

The energy of age showed. The 17-year-old headed down at a jog while my husband and I felt the decline jamming at our shins and knees. I repeatedly braced myself with the poles as we wound down around switchbacks, tracing our steps back across exposed stretches now fully engulfed in sun. I stopped to drink water.

"Guys, I'm feeling this. I need to slow down a bit, please." 'Feeling this' hardly captured the revolt stirring in my upper body. Fiery pain shot across my chest, neck and shoulders. *Take one step. Now take another one. And another.* I focused on staying upright, willing myself to move on. Surely the van couldn't be much further.

The forest provided much needed shade but also required going down the tall steps. I watched my guys nimbly drop off the small cliffs and turn to wait for me. I was falling behind. "How are you doing, Shelaine?"

"Not great," I replied, grimacing as I gingerly eased myself down the twelve-inch stair. I gasped as ground impact sent shockwaves through my torso and out the top of my head.

"What's wrong?" Bill recognized my distress. I couldn't answer.

By the time we returned to the parking lot my left shoulder, neck and jaw raged. I scrounged through my backpack, desperate for Tylenol, Advil, anything. "Eric," Bill said seriously, "we need to leave right now. Your mom is in pain."

The silence on the trip down exaggerated my urge to scream as fire shot through my upper body with every pothole bump. *Breathe. Breathe through the stabs.* "How much further?" I wasn't being funny. I stared hard out the window thinking the precipices that struck fear on the way up would be a welcome end now. *"Oh God, what have I done?"*

PART II

The Circuitous Journey

The jaw is a curious member of the body. It consists of two bones that create our mouth: the mandible, commonly known as the lower jaw, and the maxilla or upper jaw. The two sections connect in joints by the temple and both portions house our teeth. Sometimes jaw issues are medical, but mostly they are considered dental. My unique history and circumstances added mystery and complexity for both camps and led me on a four-year quest for answers.

The hiking fiasco set in motion a journey not unlike the Mt. Baker trail itself with roots to trip over, rocks to maneuver around, switchbacks that felt like a retracing of ground covered, and extended periods in the forest shade. Each step moved us closer to the summit but the grand vista was obscured by the mountain along the way. Good thing mountainsides are beautiful in their own right.

I started with my family doctor who quickly acknowledged his limited expertise in all things jaw and referred me to a local oral surgeon. "You're a clencher," pronounced the man who had met me only minutes earlier and done the briefest of examinations.

I pushed back gently. "That's strange because I don't wake up with my teeth clenched. I'm not aware of being a…"

"Well, you are," he retorted gruffly. "Reduce stress in your life. You'll be fine." Reduce stress? The persistent ache in my jaw was the source of stress, not the other way around. His report—based solely on the "open, close, open, close" assessment and no x-rays or scans—resolved: "The fact that she had temporomandibular joint surgery thirty years ago is not significant here. Shelaine will return to her dentist for fabrication of a soft night guard."

I knew the oral surgeon was wrong, but since I had no plan B, I booked an appointment with my dentist to have the appliance made.

The dental assistant took impressions of my bite. Forcing the silicone-filled trays into my restricted mouth opening caused searing pain. "Come back in two weeks," I was told. "The night guard will be ready for you." So, I did.

"Open as wide as you can and I'll slip the mouth guard in." The assistant seemed confident as she slid the formed acrylic between my teeth. I winced as her fingers ran inside my cheeks, attempting to lock the unit in place.

"That's odd," she murmured as I shrunk lower in the chair, "it doesn't seem to fit. Just a minute, please." She left and returned with the dentist who repeated her process. "I'm very sorry for your discomfort, Mrs. Strom. This isn't your night guard." Not mine? I cringed wondering whose piece of plastic had just been in my mouth. The assistant anxiously picked up the plastic bag and showed the dentist the name on it. Shelaine Strom.

"Well, this has never happened before. There must have been a mix-up at the lab. I'm really sorry for your inconvenience. We will locate your appliance and call you when this has been sorted out." They never did find it and I didn't repeat the process. I let that door stay closed.

I opened a book instead. A trusted friend had given me a copy of *Being Well When We're Ill* a few years earlier as I lost weight inexplicably before the Adrenal Insufficiency diagnosis. God has brought many books across my path at just the right time to provide counsel, shed light or to crystallize thoughts that had been twirling randomly in my head for some time. Marva Dawn's personal journey with pain and its necessary losses impacted me profoundly.

* * *

Being Well When We're Ill changed my life. The writer is a theologian who has experienced intense physical suffering and shares her path in the book. Her willingness to be authentic about the losses—and finds—inspired me. My heart's desire was to live well in the midst but I struggled to know how to do that when pain routinely rocked my world.

Of all the beneficial wisdom and support I encountered over the years, this passage perhaps shaped my ability to navigate more than any other single idea. Dawn writes:

> A first step toward finding intellectual, emotional and spiritual wellbeing in spite of the absurdity of our physical circumstances is to change the questions from "Why?" to "What?" and "Where?" and to ask these with an

open-minded commitment to look for answers. More completely, the new questions are, "What is God doing in the midst of this?" and "Where do I catch glimpses of the Trinity's grace?"

The first question is crucial because it changes the axis of our lives. We move from making ourselves the center with a focus on our own intellectual discovery of meaning or emotional relief to restoring the prominence of God in our thinking. We also shift from demanding that God provide answers to our "Why?" queries to listening for what God might want to tell us about Himself and His provisions for us.

As a result we partake in several great finds—the gifts of letting God be God in our lives, of resting in God's mysterious purposes, of humility. (*Being Well When We're Ill*, p.42)

I continued working at changing my questions and took up my calling to see God in the midst noting that, while I had no night guard in hand, I did have a referral to a Vancouver oral medicine specialist and a recommendation to have a Cone Beam scan. My dentist had enthusiastically touted the benefits of the cutting-edge technology he had recently encountered at a conference.

The upside to this imaging option, available through a private clinic, meant a short wait-time for an appointment. The downside—the 400 dollar price tag and no extended benefit coverage for this new technology. Bill and I deemed the cost worthwhile and I followed through, leaving with a CD in hand. I popped it into my computer to see nearly 600 distinct images of my jaw that meant nothing to me. Apparently I wasn't alone.

* * *

The days between appointments dragged and evidence of my increasing restrictions grew, presenting in the most basic ways.

I have always had lots of thick hair. In fact, I joked with friends that a hair appointment was more like a weight loss program as my stylist would aggressively thin my locks and drop what seemed like pounds to a mound on the floor.

In order to maintain my straight, shoulder-length look I spent at least fifteen minutes after each washing with brush in left hand and blow dryer in right pulling out the natural wave. Until I couldn't.

By Christmas of 2010 I could no longer endure the discomfort of lifting my arm to dry and straighten my hair. My look had to change, marking the first outward indicator of decline. Thankfully, curls weren't the worst expression.

* * *

In February 2011 I arrived in the office of the Oral Medicine doctor with my scan CD in hand, excited to hear news from my digital self-portrait. I sat waiting in an examination room and heard my doctor call his colleague into an office. "This is fascinating technology. Look at how this captures the mandible." My heart raced, anticipating information and perhaps even answers.

"Thanks for bringing in these images," he said, handing the disc back to me, "but neither of us know how to read them. It's very new." Not to worry, I was reassured; a bone and infection scan would help to determine if I had ongoing joint inflammatory process.

Nuclear medicine and I became intimately acquainted as radioactive dye lit up my scanned and rescanned bones. A follow up visit to the specialist in late March revealed the test results. "There is minimal evidence of infection. Assessment of the condition of the joint is obscured by the presence of metal. Images are inconclusive."

The doctor conveyed his conclusions to my family physician. "Her report is confirmed on clinical examination where increased tenderness is present in the left TM joint and extending along the posterior aspect of the zygomatic arch. There is also increased tenderness in the left masseter and temporalis regions. Due to these findings, ethyl chloride coolant spray was applied in order to assess its impact on regional pain and unfortunately, this aggravated her symptoms."

"Unfortunately, this aggravated her symptoms." I guess it's not medically sound to report, "The cold spray sent her through the roof and left her stifling the urge to vomit." He put me on a trial of systemic prednisone, noting the adverse reactions I had had to several NSAIDs (Non-steroidal Anti-inflammatory Drugs), Lyrica, Cymbalta, Codeine and Tramacet, and initiated a referral to a Vancouver oral and facial surgeon to see if removal of the image-distorting prostheses should be considered.

* * *

Each new health professional I visited required his own raft of paperwork be completed. Most blanks could be filled in with dates, treatments, and history but routinely I ran into one question I had no certain answer to: what material are the implants made of? So I began a quest to track down my original surgeon—from 31 years prior—in Phoenix. My hand shook as I dialed. The receptionist put me through to Dr. Borgeson and I introduced myself. "I remember you! You were the youngest person I operated on. How have you been?" asked the 82 year-old, still practicing doctor. I relaxed with his warmth and recollection.

I described my current situation and he offered a free over-the-phone diagnosis. "You have done really well to have been almost pain free for 30 years but it sounds like those plates need to come out now. Be careful, though. There's about a 50% chance it will make you better and 50% chance it will make you worse."

I reeled at the odds, wishing the second 50% was at least "you'll stay the same as you are now." I pulled myself back to the call's purpose and inquired about the metal.

"Titanium," he said, "at least I think that's what they were back then." I thanked him for his initial role in my life and present help. His skilled work had given me many enjoyable years.

However, his lack of certainty about the metal left me wondering, so I continued my search by calling the inventor of my prostheses. Dr. Morgan's wife answered. He had died just two months prior but she was pretty sure the plates would have been titanium. Pretty sure.

* * *

Chronic pain is exhausting, even dangerous, and my family doctor routinely checked in to ensure I wasn't becoming depressed. "How are you coping with the pain, Shelaine?" he asked.

"I use ice packs and heating pads and take Tylenol and Advil. I stay home more to avoid conversations in large groups. I walk every day and pace around the house when the intensity increases. Bill is supportive and I have compassionate friends. And, I write."

Indeed I did write. Moving feelings and thoughts to words on a screen gave release and helped me make sense of the mix inside. God gave peace and strength to persevere and I keenly felt the mounting impact of prolonged pain. Writing became my safe processing place and another means of communicating my experience with loved ones.

On April 27, 2011, at the encouragement of a counsellor, I wrote this letter to our sons.

Dear Taylor, Clark and Eric,

Recently, I have been on another journey with my health that is taking me down some paths I didn't expect nor am I delighted to be on. However, I am here and thought it might be beneficial to share some of what's going on, particularly in light of some of what may happen down the road.

You may recall the old story of me getting hit in the jaw with a baseball when I was fourteen and living in Arizona. As I reflect on the circumstances of that day now, I am quite appalled at what happened. The ball hit me hard enough to knock me completely unconscious and crack the bone fully around my chin—both directions—and crack all the way up into the mandible (the ball) in the joint. It also punctured the cartilage. The bizarre part to me is that 911 was not called. My parents were not notified and I walked home from school alone. Only days later did I find out about the broken bones.

What was not evident with those initial x-rays was that the punctured cartilage formed a donut-like ring of scar tissue that prevented the jaw from opening and caused excruciating pain. I spent the next nine months living on intense painkillers, eating mush and wondering if I'd ever open my mouth again.

After a serious reaction to some of the drugs I was on, the surgeon decided I was too young to be on such powerful pain medication and he performed surgery. I was his youngest patient ever and I'm ever so grateful for the work he did. He removed the damaged tissue and did what, at the time, was the best thing to do. He replaced the cartilage with metal plates that are screwed into my cheek bones.

Today, this surgery would never be performed. The medical profession knows so much more about the jaw joint and how different it is from other joints. You simply can't treat it like a hip or knee. So, the good news is I have had over 30 years with these implants. From the research I've done, many people had to have them removed after only 3–5 years, due to pain and joint dysfunction. The courts are full of litigation surrounding this controversial procedure as some people had Teflon plates and that's just nasty. Thankfully, all evidence points to mine being metal without a Teflon coating.

Now fast forward 30 years. I am experiencing ever-increasing pain and limited mobility in my jaw. The left side is particularly bad. I have lived in and with pain for the last

15+ years, but only within the last year has it become more localized to the jaw area. This last fall, I think something was further injured during a hike I did. I don't know for sure but the intensity of pain has grown consistently since that period of time.

It seems that the jaw may be the culprit or root issue in many health things I deal with. I have numerous autoimmune symptoms which may very well be a sign of my body rejecting these "foreign" materials in my head. Seems strange after all these years but, as I look back, it's been developing over time.

Also, and this one I hate to actually admit, but there is a very real possibility that I have a screw loose! You may have already had that figured out… ☺ Truly, it seems likely that one or both of the screws in the plate on the left side may have shifted and may account for the intensity of pain in that bone area. The difficulty we're facing is that there is no way to image the joint. Anything X ray-like ends up with a great deal of distortion from the metal in there. The only thing that really displays the joint effectively anyway is an MRI. Let's ponder that thought for a moment….Magnetic Resonance Imaging. Magnetic….metal in head…. that would be one quick way to get the plates out….no thanks.

So now I'm waiting for a surgical consult. It would seem like a no-brainer that we should just take these implants out and be done with it all. Unfortunately, it's not that simple. Every entry into this joint causes trauma, scar tissue, and further nerve and muscle damage. What it would do is allow the jaw to realign properly and hopefully inflammation would be reduced. They would clean out the joint and give it a "fresh start." The odds I've been given at this point are 50/50. There seems to be no neutral outcome—meaning it will make life much better or much worse. Now there's a decision to make!

And that really is the purpose of this letter. I stand very close to the threshold of having to make a decision that could have serious ramifications for my future and the amount of pain I live with. So, I'm asking that you join with me to pray for discernment, clarity and wisdom.

Perhaps it is for another letter another day, but I want you to know that I believe that God is capable of healing this completely. I believe that God does heal today. And, I believe that it is entirely God's right to heal or not, as He sees fit. If there is anything I have learned on this health journey, it's that I see such a small portion of the picture. God's vision is perfect, mine so limited. I choose to trust Him.

I'm reading a book right now by a woman who became a quadriplegic at seventeen. She had prayed for healing for years and God's answer has consistently been "no." I relate very much to what she has learned and she says it well in this passage:

> A no answer has purged sin from my life, strengthened my commitment to Him, forced me to depend on grace, bound me with other believers, produced discernment, fostered sensitivity, disciplined my mind, taught me to spend my time wisely...and widened my world beyond

what I would have ever dreamed…My affliction has stretched my hope, made me know Christ better, helped me long for truth, led me to repentance of sin, goaded me to give thanks in times of sorrow, increased my faith and strengthened my character. …[Illness] has meant knowing Him better, feeling His pleasure every day.

(*A Place of Healing: Wrestling with the Mysteries of Suffering, Pain, and God's Sovereignty*, Joni Eareckson Tada)

I would, of course, be most grateful if God should choose to heal and free me of pain. But I do not want to miss the miracle of healing that God does every day in my life. There is so much more to healing than release from physical symptoms. I have often told my class in relation to my health journey, "I wouldn't wish it on anyone. I wouldn't want to do it again. I wouldn't change it for anything." God has taken these physical issues and used them to grow me and to accomplish His purposes. I'm good with that. And I am seeking the Lord, not healing. I am seeking His best, not what I think is best. And I am willing to surrender to whatever His plan is.

And so I ask you, my wonderful sons, to join with me in discerning what His plan is. I will continue to walk through the medical steps and ask that as I walk, the path before me will be lit and the way become clear.

Thanks to each of you for being you. I love you all.

Mom

* * *

And in private I wrote:

> What a lonely place pain is. Friends can send encourage-
> ment notes, freely give hugs and empathy. But I walk this
> road of pain alone, in many respects. You can't share pain
> or give a portion of it to someone else to carry for a while.
> Pain is my constant companion and it's not a friendly or
> comforting one. Joni wrote that as pain increases, God
> pulls me harder into His embrace. What does that really
> feel like? God, are you pulling me into your embrace? Can
> I feel you holding me in spite of the searing pain through
> my cheek bone or the punishing pressure through the side
> of my face? What does the embrace of God really feel like?
> I know in theory that I'm not alone—that He will nev-
> er leave or forsake me. And in my head, I rehearse that
> truth regularly. But I feel alone. I feel disconnected from
> my family, from friends, from everything. I live inside my
> throbbing head, aware of the need to stay in the present,
> frighteningly aware that the future is uncertain and may
> include even more pain. I do not for a moment believe that
> I know pain and suffering like I may come to know it. I am
> well aware that there is always more pain awaiting and that
> no one, no one else, can bear it or carry it or live with it but
> me. I want to believe that God will give me the strength, as
> He has to this point, to bear the pain. And, I also know that
> I am growing weary. I tire of waking in pain, living all day
> in pain, going to bed in pain and being wakened through
> the night by pain. Constant companion is no exaggeration.
> I am not alone. My friend pain is with me all the time.

* * *

The medical intake forms I routinely completed also asked me to rate my pain on a scale of 1-10. Annoyance rose in me each time I was forced to circle a simple number while pain grew, slowly and methodically stripping away my life.

How can those losses and feelings be reduced to one digit? Documents at the oral and facial surgeon's office in June of 2011 were no different. I completed them while Bill and I sat in the waiting room surrounded by before-and-after pictures of plastic-looking, hyper-happy people sporting new faces and teeth. Perhaps that should have been a clue.

The assistant showed me to the dental chair and began a series of questions, interjecting routinely. "What kind of work do you do?" She interrupted my reply with, "At least you can still work! You should see some of our patients."

"Well, it's getting much harder to work because I'm an instructor and…"

Again she jumped in, "You've got it good. You can still talk. Some of our patients can't even do that."

I sat in stunned silence. She carried on, "You need to stay with this doctor. He's really good. Don't go traipsing around looking for answers. There are a lot of quacks out there who will cut off your bones and leave you worse off than you are now. You're really not doing that badly. Oh, here's the doctor."

I felt relieved when the surgeon joined us and the assistant quit talking.

"What kind of pain do you have?" he asked.

Flustered by the preceding barrage I sat silently trying to compose myself and find words other than, "the kind that hurts." He grew impatient.

With pursed lips and piercing eyes he challenged, "How can I accurately diagnose your condition if you can't describe it to me? Is the pain aching, gnawing, burning, sharp, shooting, sickening, splitting, stabbing, throbbing, exhausting, continuous, intermittent? And how do you rank the pain on a scale of 1-10, 1 being hardly noticeable and 10 being the worst pain you have ever experienced?"

"Umm, it's all of those at different times, I think."

"Which pain do you have most often and how intense is it?" I stumbled around my answers still thrown by the earlier news that I "wasn't doing that badly" compared to other patients.

"You need to be clearer with your descriptions if we are going to be able to help you," he admonished, his assistant nodding in smug agreement.

I blurted out more words as he prepared for his diagnostic procedure. "I will inject freezing into three different areas of your joint. Once the anesthetic hits the pain-producing region you will feel relief and I will know the source of your pain." He was correct. Sort of.

He inserted the first and second needles in front of my ear and little changed. The third injection directly entered the joint, stopping abruptly with a crunch and then, blissfully, I felt nothing. "Okay, I have the information I need. Come back in two weeks."

I paid the nine hundred dollar bill and left with a smile, numb and painless for the first time in months and headed across the street with Bill for sushi.

The time it took for our lunch to arrive corresponded precisely with how long it took the freezing to wear off. Unwittingly, I bit down on my California roll and searing stabs shot through my joint and into my temple. We left the restaurant as I gasped for air, fending off passing out, neither of us even thinking that we could go back to the surgeon's office. Instead, Bill drove home while I moaned and scoured my purse for Tylenol, Advil, anything. It would be three years before I bit into anything harder than a ripe peach.

Not only had I lost my ability to bite through food but my pain soared to new heights and I wrestled with how to live with it. I wrote to a trusted friend:

> In the biggest sense, I know that I will be fine. Today, I'm not fine. Today I'm in pain to the point of nausea and despair to the point of giving up the quest for relief. I give in. I quit. I lose. It's not for me to have relief from this pain in this world, I think. So, I'm not going chasing after anything anymore. I will do my best to live with what I have, without whining, but I will not spend the little energy I have chasing the wind. I will not make more appointments with any doctors or dentists. I will cancel what I currently have and just let it be what it is. If God has something else in mind, I'm listening. Right now I'm not hearing anything beyond the voice of "quit." So, I quit. I officially resign from the path of seeking pain management. Call it navigating, call it management, call it whatever you like. It doesn't work and I'm not doing it anymore.
>
> Please don't ask me anymore how I'm doing physically. I'm not going to talk about it, give it attention it doesn't deserve, or dwell on it any more. I am, in effect, going to try

living in denial for a while and see if it makes a difference. Perhaps the idea that the thought precedes the feeling can be helpful here. I choose not to think about the pain. I hope not to feel the pain...

I'm not saying I want to die. Quite the opposite, actually. I want to live. That's my problem. I want to live and have life and have it without restraint and caution and pain. I just feel left on the sidelines and that the world is going to carry on without me. I'll be alone in my pain, just like I am right now.

* * *

A month after the ill-fated injections a fellow guest at a wedding reception asked, "What kind of crazy diet are you on?" observing my choice of mashed potatoes and Jell-O from the bounty of the buffet.

"It's because of my jaw," I replied, weary of explaining, exhausted by the previous month of highest ever soreness and greater dietary limitations. I really didn't want to talk about it. But she did. "What happened? How did you get to this point? Who have you seen? How often are you in pain? How does it affect your life?" I excused myself to pick up a dessert I didn't want just for a reprieve. She persisted and by the end of the meal I'd agreed to let her discuss my case with her husband, an orthodontist. I hoped that would be the end of it.

He called within a week and after hearing my story concluded, "Shelaine, no one should live in as much pain as you have. It's not safe." He told me of two chronic pain sufferers he knew who had taken their own lives. The reality jolted me.

He offered to call his friend, a jaw surgeon in Vancouver, and plead my case. I agreed.

The surgeon said no. "I'm sorry, Shelaine, but Dr. M. won't take you as a patient because he doesn't regularly perform the procedure you require." My orthodontist friend took a breath as I expelled all oxygen from my lungs. "And he emphasized that you should not let anyone touch your jaw unless they do nothing but TMJ surgery and there are only two of those surgeons in Canada. He gave me the name of the one in Edmonton."

Do I pursue this? Do I give up? Oh, God, what do I do? July 16, 2011, I wrote:

> Be merciful to me, O Lord, for I am in distress; my eyes grow weak with sorrow, my soul and my body with grief. My life is consumed by anguish and my years by groaning, my strength fails because of my affliction, and my bones grow weak. Because of all my enemies, I am the utter contempt of my neighbors; I am a dread to my friends—those who see me on the street flee from me. I am forgotten by them as though I am dead. I have become like broken pottery. For I hear the slander of many, there is terror on every side; they conspire against me and plot to take my life.
>
> But I trust in you, O Lord; I say, "You are my God." My times are in your hands; deliver me from my enemies and from those who pursue me. Let your face shine on your servant; save me in your unfailing love. (Psalm 31: 9-16)
>
> What if this is as good as it gets?
>
> Be merciful to me, God. I am in distress. Pain is my constant companion. I sit and think of going away to rest but I know that I will go with me. I know that pain goes

with me and seeps into everything. It clouds all I do and say and how I see. My eyes grow weak with sorrow. I am tired of seeing a blurred version of life. How ironic that my sight is literally blurring and becoming so poor. I cannot read most things now without glasses and to wear glasses is to put pressure on my jaw. Nothing is unaffected. My eyes grow weary with sorrow.

My strength fails because of my affliction. I have taught one day and I feel my strength lessened as it used to be after the whole week of teaching. My capacity to bounce back is so small now. My ability to do anything beyond the essentials shrinks regularly. I want to lash out. I want to scream and rail and cry about the injustice and the unfairness and I don't. Because I know at the core of my being that this isn't personal. It just is. I am broken pottery in a world full of shards and pieces and the very best I can hope for is that the Potter will be merciful. That the Potter's hands will reach into my scattered remains and hold the segments—tenderly gather the bits and fragments and provide some means of restoration. There are pieces missing now, I'm sure. Some parts have been crushed to fine powder and have no form to glue back together. That leaves gaps—some might call them mysteries. The places that have no relief, no answers, more questions. Broken pottery. Today the pieces lay in disarray, with no apparent form or meaning. Shards and sharp edges protrude.

But I trust in You, O Lord. Do I? Can I really trust that You are good and You know me fully? Can I believe that you created my inmost being? That You were there the day the ball struck me and changed the course of my life? Were You there? Where are You now? I look for You each day and I see You but do You see me? Do You see what I'm missing in life and relationship because this pain continues? Do You see how small and narrow my life has become? Do You see me? Do You see the decisions I am forced to make that exclude me from living and from people? Do You see how I disappoint others because I can't be who I used to be? Do You see how I choose over and over again to believe? It's hard. I want to believe You are good and sovereign and trustworthy. I do. It's hard right now.

In my alarm I said, "I am cut off from your sight!" Yet you heard my cry for mercy when I called to you for help....Be strong and take heart, all you who hope in the Lord. (Psalm 31: 22,24)

* * *

I know God was behind the renewed commitment to press on for relief but on a human level it also had to do with that acquaintance taking up my cause. The orthodontist's care and willingness to advocate for me mattered.

I was ready to resume my push for answers and booked an appointment with my family doctor who graciously wrote yet another letter of referral. By the end of September 2011, "Dr. Edmonton" had me on his waitlist for an initial consultation. I was told not to expect to see him for over two years.

But something shifted through this experience, perhaps with the knowledge that a work was in progress, or maybe it came from the glimpse I began to have of God behind the scenes directing my steps. Shortly after being put on the long list, I journaled an entry I called *Acceptance*:

> I went to visit a friend the other day as she waits at home for procedures and answers to her health concerns. As we chatted, she asked if I had heard from Dr. Edmonton, as we have come to refer to him.
>
> After replying, no, I hadn't and that I had no intention of contacting them until after my work ended, she came back with this quick reply. "You know what's going to happen, don't you? You are going to finish work, Dr. Edmonton will call and you'll go there and get this all sorted out and then be able to get on with your life."
>
> Immediately I felt an internal reaction of resistance and dislike for her comments. I responded with something about needing to live life and not just wait. Then I also told her I might not even choose to have surgery. Her non-verbal response would indicate she didn't like that possibility very much.
>
> Generally speaking, I don't think we humans are very good with uncertainty or the unknown or waiting or accepting that pain happens. After meeting with my counsellor the other day, I am reminded that I am choosing to live my life—each day—for what it holds. I'm not choosing to put everything on hold until I hear from this doctor. In fact, I can feel within myself a willingness to accept that this may be the life I am given to live and there may be no surgery or pill or procedure that will fix it. These are the very circumstances of my life—certainly for this stage—and maybe forever. I am okay with that.

* * *

The thing about chronic pain is that life carries on around you, requiring daily choices for how to live. I earned a PhD equivalent in weighing and measuring as I routinely evaluated opportunities and requirements through a filter of values. *Yes, I want to attend my son's jazz concert. An evening event. High pitched notes. People I'll know will want to talk in that noisy room. Jaw muscles will seize. Joints will scream. Won't sleep well for two or three nights. Can I afford to do this? Can I afford not to?*

* * *

"I don't like how my issues are affecting people I love," I declared to my counselor. "I can't be who I used to be and I feel like my husband and kids and friends are paying a price for that as well."

"Will you choose to trust God enough to let these life circumstances be part of the work He is doing in the lives of the people you love?"

His response cut to the heart of my fears. Maybe I could free myself and let go of the expectations I have of me. Maybe.

The angst over disappointing my people slowly abated.

* * *

February 9, 2012, I wrote:

"Hey, hon, how was your night?" Bill inquired warmly.

"Typical. Saw every hour. Couldn't find a comfortable position."

"Well, at least you aren't taking sleeping pills."

I walked away, stunned, and showered.

Later I joined Bill at the fireplace. "William, what does that statement about sleeping pills represent for you?" Before he could answer I added, "Because it feels pretty judgmental to me, like requiring medication to sleep would be some sort of 'less than, not trying hard enough, cop-out.'"

"No, it's not that at all. I just don't want to see you have to have an addiction added to all the things you have to deal with."

So there's the fear. I called it something like "I don't want my wife to be a pill junky." The discussion dipped and turned but I feel like the medication part is sorted through well enough.

The part that astounds me is his line of questions. "Would you say your pain has increased in the last six months? Three months? One month?" Each of the questions was answered with a resounding "yes!" And, it increased again in this week, thanks to the pressure allergy congestion puts on my cheek bones.

And then came the zinger, the statement that made the emotional expenditure in the conversation worthwhile. "I'm sure you've said things about it along the way but it's been lost on me."

That's the nugget I must take away and hold tightly to. He is not being devastated daily by my pain. He is not continually wrestling with God about the absence of his wife, due to pain. He doesn't even notice or track or take in, at a deep level, what this life of pain really is.

Part of me wants to scream and sees much more clearly why I feel invisible at times and part of me is profoundly relieved. I am not disappointing him regularly. I am not holding him back or leaving him feeling hard done by. In fact, if anything, he appears to be living life, largely feeling unaffected by my struggle.

Is it a grace given by God? Is it denial? Am I not speaking loudly enough? What a mystery this is.

* * *

I loved my career. Those 17+ years I walked with people in work and life transitions transformed me as I partnered with like-minded teammates who desired to show Christ's love to each participant. I learned about listening and the power of story as I watched even the crustiest of clients relent when offered a safe place to share their experiences and be supported. For years I thrived with the meaningful opportunities to be a small part of people's healing journey through both instruction and individual client meetings.

But pain crept in and stole joy. Each sentence I spoke yanked at rope-tight masseters. Laughing shot spikes through temples. I winced and held the side of my face trying not to draw attention to my condition. My six-hour teaching days, which used to fly by with engaged interaction, dragged. *Only 10 minutes until break. I've almost made it to lunch and then only another two hours. I can do this. I think.*

In early 2012, I met with a client for his individual coaching session after the group aspect of the program had been completed. We discussed his take-aways from the course and next steps. As the meeting drew to a close he thanked me and said, "It's nice to finally get to interact with you. In the class, you're like a rock star. You show up, perform and disappear before we have a chance to talk to you." His assessment burned true. It hadn't always been that way. I no longer had the capacity to serve my clients as I used to. I struggled to make it through each day.

Spring of 2012 marked the end of the government contract for Success@Work. Perhaps I would have taken a medical leave sooner if our entire program were not drawing to a close. I saw March as a natural place to pull back, if only I could get there.

February 16, 2012, I wrote:

I've just completed my second-to-last day of teaching interview skills. It was painful. The class is small and, while seemingly interested in the topic, they remain largely uncommunicative and exceptionally beige. I couldn't get through the day fast enough and can hardly tolerate the thought of going and doing it all over again tomorrow.

Is this a gift? Will the ending of this chapter of my life be so welcomed by the time I reach it that I won't look back or long for what was? I can hardly believe it possible and I can hardly wait. This is not the job I loved.

Change happens. I know that. I teach that. I try to embrace that. I seem to be recognizing within myself that I am a clinger. I hold on till the bitter end—I go down with the Titanic. It has seemed a virtue of sorts in the past—the loyal thing to do. But I'm questioning that now and those fellow employees who were the "ship-jumpers" perhaps

had the better plan. They are gone from this death by terminal illness and initiated their own clean end. Sure it was
hard and I know they miss us. But this is really hard.

I want to finish well. That matters to me and I am committed to it. I believe in closure. And, it may just suck the
very last ounce of life out of me to do it. What am I doing?

The future is such a mix. There will be great relief in
being set free from the routine of Success@Work. How
many years have I been governed by the program's calendar? No two weeks in a month are the same. Rarely are
two months in a row the same.

I'll have all this freedom and what's left of me to enjoy
it? I think that's the biggest uncertainty for me at the moment. Freedom—countless days of no schedule, no routine, no accountability. April feels like a swear word. It's
that empty void I will have to enter into, face and come out
the other side.

What do I do next? I can go on medical Employment
Insurance and just take 3–4 months completely off. If I do
that, will I lose the momentum of private contacts? Will
I rest and give my jaw a break and find some strength to
move ahead? Do I go back to school in the fall and work
toward a Masters? Should I take my coaching certification
and make a concerted effort to build that business?

And I know the answer to that, too. God, I know that
You know and I am to trust. Just do the next thing. Take
the next step. See where it all goes. I am actually quite at
peace with that. Or maybe I'm just exhausted from all the
"carrying on." I keep taking the next step and doing the
next thing and I'm weary. I need a break.

* * *

All of my work required my mouth. Projecting to a crowd engaged facial muscles connected to jaw muscles attached to broken-down joints. Coaching one person in a quiet office resulted in less sharp attacks but drew intensely on and sucked away my fading energies. I pushed hard to finish well, knowing our contract would be fulfilled, the office would close, and our entire team would be unemployed. While the others made plans to move to a next job, I anticipated quitting everything.

* * *

March 11, 2012, I read the following Artway Devotional by Juliet Benner on Jean-François Millet: The Angelus (1857–1859):

> The painting presents two peasants in a field near the close of day. We see the faint outline of a city behind them in the distance. This is a moment of deep and quiet reverence. All work has abruptly stopped as both the man and the woman stand in bowed silence. The man, hat in hand, stands in devout humility and worship. The woman also bows her head, her hands tightly clasped in prayer close to her chest. It is an intensely private moment for each of them, yet their shared prayer unites them together in a holy alliance where God is present...
>
> Everything in this work invites us to stillness and meditation. The figures are immobile. The tools of their trade are abandoned. The landscape is completely flat and there is no movement at all, except for the barely visible birds in

the distant sky. Time almost seems to stand still, and we become aware that this moment is special and sacred. For these people of prayer, with the eyes of their heart turned toward God, the world has grown dim, dissolved in heavenly light. The blaze of light behind them, symbolic of the radiant glory of God, seems to transfuse their humble daily tasks with dignity and nobility.

My response:

I am struck by the timing of receiving this devotional, and, more specifically, awareness of this piece of art. This couple is stopping their work and responding to the sound of bells as a reminder to pray. The connection seems applicable to my life stage as I believe God has intervened—the bells are ringing —and my work at Strategic is ending. But there is a deeper application as well. I am choosing to stop and pay closer attention to God—not just with the ending of Success@Work, but also for all my private work. I am setting aside not just my basket but my garden hoe, my pitchfork, my watering can. I am making a commitment to not working for the purpose of healing, strengthening, discovering, reacquainting myself with God, myself and others.

The stoppage of work to pray when the bells ring is an intentional act. I want to be intentional with my work stoppage as well. I desire the time to be one of rest and refreshment, of assessment of what I really can and cannot do, perhaps even what I should or should not do.

I want to enter into this time with a posture of openness and expectation, not loss and sorrow. I catch glimpses of what could be—only fleeting ideas or possibilities. And, in faith, I choose to stop work. I choose to believe that the One who has sounded the bell to end the contract is also the One who will give direction, provisions, new opportunities. I will stop and pray and wait.

* * *

Days off were spent reeling and recovering from days on. Life narrowed to little more than work and pain management. Bill and I spent our together-time watching hockey in the evenings, quietly. I sat on the floor. He rubbed my shoulders and neck, graciously attempting to lessen my desire to crawl out of my skin.

* * *

End well. Finish strong. Be that employee that goes above and beyond.

The tenuous balance of providing excellent service and program delivery to our clients while navigating my own grief process stretched my capacities. My position as team leader called loudly to my "responsible self" and I determined to walk our team to a positive conclusion. I purposed to end well.

During our last month in operation, I led as we sorted our way through copious numbers of pens and hordes of stationery. We hauled boxes out of storage and distributed materials into 'garbage', 'thrift shop' and 'keep it' categories. Our boss empowered me to make decisions freely and we slowly wrapped up a season of life and work.

Over the years, my role in the company encompassed many unofficial titles and I loosely wore the hat of techy-person. To be clear, my involvement in the technology side of work-life mostly consisted of buying new computers and knowing who to call when they didn't behave. I had, however, paid close attention to the service person's work and asked lots of questions. So, when it came time to wipe the classroom laptops of confidential information and prepare them for sale, I did the job with ease.

After cleaning eight student laptops, my confidence soared —probably in direct correlation to my fatigue and desire to be done. I successfully wiped one instructor office machine and began with the next one.

"Shelaine! The resume I saved only seconds ago is gone. It vanished right before my eyes. Something is very wrong!" My co-worker, Sue, reported frantically at my office door.

I froze. I gasped as the possibility sank in. Turning back to the screen, the nausea-inducing suspicion confirmed itself. This computer, not the one out front, was our network administrator. Those 'local files' I deleted really began wiping the entire system.

Breathe in, breathe out, I counseled myself. *Think. What would Dave say to do?* I had learned from Dave, the generous, teacher-hearted IT guy, that rule number one in a computer crisis states: "Do not panic and push buttons or try things." Apparently only having to address the initial issue is easier than having to undo all the repair attempts. *How could I have done this? What was I thinking?*

"What did you do?" Sue prodded, observing my green face.

"This computer," I stammered, "I deleted...I thought it was only this machine...I forgot about it being the network one...oh my goodness, what else have I gotten rid of?"

Optimistically Sue asked, "You should be able to undo it, shouldn't you?" just as Tanya arrived at my door announcing, "Shelaine, I can't find the accounting files. It's like they've vanished. I just used them this morning." *Seriously? All the financial records of the company evaporated at my touch?*

Groans poured out in tandem with the clunk of my head on the desk. *How could it have come to this? It matters so much to me to finish well and I've just blown it. Who is this person making this unbelievably stupid mistake? I knew this was the network machine. How could I have forgotten that? Okay, think girl. How do you handle this?*

"I need to call our server guy and see if he can access the backups. I'm really sorry this is interrupting your work. Please pray he can restore everything."

Steve arrived, assessed the situation and left with the promise of giving it his best shot and the disturbing warning not to get my hopes up. Apparently my capacity for deleting ranked as thorough and excellent—not exactly what I hoped to add to my resume.

For three hours I battled inwardly trying not to create every possible worst case scenario. At 5:30, the phone rang and Steve announced he had recovered the lost material, he thought. It was possible a few gaps existed but for the most part, he had retrieved the contents. Had he been in the building, I would have hugged him. Instead, we women shared a group hug and I finally exhaled.

My boss and fellow staff extended grace but I felt deeply disappointed in myself. My desire to be a model employee had superseded an accurate assessment of my pain-ravaged cognitive capacities. I was the human example of the story I told many clients. If you drop a frog into boiling water he will jump out immediately to save his life. If you put a frog in cold water and slowly raise the temperature to boiling, he will die. Too much pain. Too long. A slow boil.

On March 29, 2012, the office doors officially closed. Unemployed. My new title.

* * *

A friend from Arizona days invited me and my friend Sue to spend a week at her place in Mesa, the city where my jaw journey began. One of our first day trips included revisiting the ball diamond. We parked at the back of the school property on the edge of the field and began a prayer walk around the bases, asking God to release me from anything that could hinder my attitude and healing going forward. Sue asked if I held any bitterness toward the coach and, while I had no awareness of that, I asked God to show me if I did. We ended with quiet reflection sitting in the dugout and then moved to the air conditioned car as the morning temperature climbed into the 90's.

Sue began reading an article she brought for this moment, interrupted by a sharp tap on my window. With a start I turned into the peering down face of the school security guard.

"This is a closed campus, ma'am. You are not allowed here without permission. What is the purpose of you being here?" he asked sternly.

"Oh, I'm so sorry. I didn't even think of that," I stammered. "I went to school here years ago and wanted to show my friend. We're visiting from Canada."

He didn't look convinced. "May I see your driver's license?" As he walked away with it he added, "You'll have to wait here until the police arrive." Sue and I exchanged raised eyebrows and big eyes as the policeman pulled his cruiser directly behind my rear bumper. We really weren't going anywhere.

Minutes before we had been laughing over my alteration of a sign posted on the chain link in front of us which read, "No hitting, pitching, or throwing balls against any fence." With my hand over the "en" in fence it read "face." I decided not to share the story with the officer when he returned my license.

He gave grace, explaining that legally he could strip search us and our car but that he wouldn't. Instead, he stated firmly, "Ma-am, you don't belong here." No, I don't. That chapter of life is over. Things happen and, although I had felt freedom over the years, this encounter confirmed my commitment to continue looking forward.

* * *

During the earlier quest to confirm my prosthetic's composition I scoured the internet and found a study being done at the University of Minnesota on people who had undergone TMJ implant surgery, just like the arthroplasty I had undergone. The goal of their research was to determine the long-term success of the procedure and to collect any removed implants. I signed up to be a participant and promptly forgot about it.

Almost a year later, in March of 2012, I phoned to find that funding had been cut and the project shelved. My heart sank. I wanted to be part of a club with people just like me instead of bearing anomaly status. My silent disappointment must have been audible because the woman shifted to asking if I knew that the U of M had a TMD (temporomandibular disorders) and Orofacial Pain clinic. Initially she offered an appointment six to eight months down the road then said, "Wait, I just had a cancellation for June 7th. Would you like it?"

Would I like an appointment the day before our nephew's Minnesota wedding that we had been planning to attend for six months? Would I like to see a team of specialists in Minneapolis with expertise like I had yet to encounter, 1400 miles from our home, the day after our flight lands in that city on tickets purchased three months ago? Would I like to be assessed in two months instead of the 18-24 month wait for Dr. Edmonton?

"Yes. I would like that appointment, please."

* * *

Expectations ran high as Bill and I entered the Dentistry building on the University of Minnesota campus. We knew that countless people were praying for us and we felt nervously excited at the potential for answers. Armed with my folder of reports, test results, and a still un-interpreted Cone Beam scan, we made our way to the fourth floor. Little did we know it would be a three-hour stay.

The clinic is part of the teaching school so I quickly became acquainted with the specialist and three of his students, one of whom conducted the initial interview, asking pages of questions. She also did an examination and took copious notes as I gave lists of symptoms, restrictions and a general life impact statement. After she concluded her part, the rest of the team joined us.

"What do you see here on the lower gum?" asked the specialist. Six other eyes peered into my mouth while doing the dental survey. "I don't see any notation about this. It could be an early indication of oral cancer. Have you asked the patient about the history of the spot?"

'The patient' squirmed and then offered, "It's a mark I've had on my gum since I had a root canal done over 15 years ago. It's always looked like that and hasn't changed over time."

"That's right, because it's an amalgam tattoo. But we can't conclude that without exploring the history with the patient. Clear?" Yes, we were all clear on that issue.

"So you brought a Cone Beam scan with you, I hear. Where is the report?" Dr. Schiffman asked.

"Good question," I joked. "In fact, I've been carrying this CD around from appointment to appointment and no one can read it. Can you?"

"No, but I know who can. I'll be right back."

The TMJ specialist left me in the examination room with the three young women, all dental school graduates now studying TMJ disorders. I broke the awkward silence by asking how they came to be specializing in jaw issues.

"I don't like general dentistry so I think this will be better. I don't like looking in people's mouths," one replied.

Had my jaw been able to drop, it would have. "You don't like looking in people's mouths? How did you ever find your way into dental school?"

"It's what my parents want me to do. I am too afraid to disappoint them."

Note to self. Life is too short to make major choices based on not disappointing others.

And with that, he was back with the results. "You have metal prostheses in your TM joints."

It's with statements like that that I struggle to keep my cheeky remarks silenced. I wanted to say, "Seriously? How could that have happened? I had no idea!"

He didn't stop there.

"They are malpositioned, meaning they have moved since your original surgery, which has caused severe degenerative joint disease. Your joints have multiple osteophytes. There is also extensive nerve damage and muscle involvement as well."

I drew in oxygen slowly. Osteophytes, the stalagmites and stalactites of joints, produced by over 30 years of bone rubbing on metal, were stabbing into my tissues and preventing full range of motion. No wonder it hurt so much. The news I had waited for wasn't good but at least I was talking with someone in the know. "So what does all of that mean?" I dared ask.

"We will put together a multi-dimensional treatment plan…" His words trailed into my relief that he could do something for me. I began tracking again with, "…and I'll refer you to our surgeon for a consult to see if the best course is removal of the implants."

I left the office that day with an appointment to return to Minnesota in two months. I sent an email with these thoughts to our prayer team.

"As strange as it may seem given what I was told yesterday, difficult news is actually easier to live with than floundering around in pain, uncertainty and ignorance. While I definitely would have been happy with a quick fix or easy answer, I know that the same sovereign God who has provided for and cared for me to this point won't leave me now. I am thankful for the hope of at least some possible pain reduction and future treatment options."

And with that, we flew back home to BC with a prescription for my new friend, the pain patch.

I've never been a particularly vain person, one overly concerned with my appearance, and I'd also never been required to stick a one inch square of medicated white gauze over my left jaw joint. But pain overrode pride and I applied a new patch each morning, thankful for the numbing effect that took my levels down a notch or two. I chose to view my adornment as the 'cast' I had long wished for so others could see my injury. It didn't exactly turn out to be that, more often drawing stares, perplexed looks and curious questions.

One Sunday after our church service I darted into the coffee area to locate my husband. I wanted to leave, now. A man very familiar with my jaw situation intercepted me as I made my way through the crowd. "What's that on your face?" he inquired. "Is that a nicotine patch?" I forced a smile and replied, "No, a pain patch" and disengaged. As I retreated I wished I had said, *No, but if I ever should need a nicotine patch I'll be sure to wear it on my face!*, confirming my belief that many times it was better for me not to speak.

* * *

It was time to face the reality of our financial situation.

In late May 2012 I wrote:

My sinuses hammered on my forehead, threatening to burst through bone and skin. My abdomen tightened, back ached and intestines gurgled. My jaw burned and shot red hot stabs into my temple. The day starts here. What does one look forward to in a day that begins like this?

And then my disability application arrived. It appeared as if someone had haphazardly grabbed the necessary documents and shoved them into the envelope. These papers that could determine a significant portion of my future weren't even folded neatly, likely compiled in just a few seconds. The worker did it all the time. A meaningless task for him or her, perhaps. Me? Applying for disability? Is this real?

Supper happens, dishes are done, a friend recovering in our home from day surgery is doing better than any of us expected. And I am falling apart. Piece by piece, I am scattered about, unclear of where to go, how to be. I watch hockey, praying that will dull the pain. It's a "crawl out of my skin" night—the worst to have anyone around for. I'm not the model hostess/nurse. I'm kind. I do the necessary acts of kindness. I always do. And then I go to bed and cry myself to sleep wondering, when will someone see that I am not well? When will I see it?

I just want a casserole.

*   *   *

Completing the application for federal disability pension took paperwork to a whole new level. Documents needed to be filed to give approval for physicians to release my medical records. My physician was required to file trees-worth of information and compile countless test results, the final submission tallying over 40 pages.

My contribution was no less involved. During this process, Bill and I were gifted with free accommodations on Vancouver Island. The home sat perched on a mountain edge overlooking Cowichan Bay, a million dollar view. Everything about the location shouted beauty as I slogged through the application mire. "Explain any difficulties/functional limitations you have with the following:"

Lifting—If I lift a gallon of milk, my shoulder pain increases immediately resulting in increased, sharp jaw pain. *I used to do all the grocery shopping. Now I can only buy a few light-weight items.*

Driving—If I drive for more than 15 minutes, my hip and shoulder pain increases. Need to take frequent breaks to walk and move. *When the boys were little we did 36-hour road trips to visit Bill's parents. Now I can't drive 25 minutes to Langley without serious repercussions.*

Concentrating—Inability to sit and focus due to pain decreases concentration. Sharp pain interrupts thoughts and task focus. Easily distracted. *I used to be able to read for hours or listen to speakers with keen attention. Now I can hardly wait for every event to be over.*

Sleeping—Rolling onto my left side in my sleep results in

immobility due to sharpness of pain. Sleep is routinely interrupted by muscle and joint pain. *And my husband has to sleep next door because I spend the night fidgeting, in search of comfort. My bed is full of pillows to prop body parts and nothing helps for more than half an hour.*

Household maintenance—Cleaning—Can only wipe counter tops, do dishes. No heavy cleaning or reaching like cleaning a bathtub requires. *I just turned 47, not 87. This is pathetic.*

The list went on as I struggled to articulate how every aspect of my world was touched. 'Can't do's' piled up. 'No longer able to's' screamed from the page.

From across the room Bill asked, "Hey would you like to drive over to the marina and explore that area this afternoon?"

"NO! I can't. I'm too sore and too tired and I can't do it. Just like everything else in my life right now. I can't, can't, can't. I can't even wear glasses anymore," and with that, I threw them across the room. "I. Don't. Want. *This*. Life!" I screamed.

Bill sat in stunned silence while I paced, tears flooding. Eventually he came toward me, warily, and reached out. I wept angry tears as he held me for a long time. "I'm sorry for losing it. I just don't want to live like this for the rest of my life. I hate it on every level."

The outburst did nothing to alter the course I needed to follow. In fact, on some levels it added stress as I internalized shame that I couldn't handle the situation more maturely. I believed my husband saw the flare-ups as a failure, adding to my sense of not living up to some standard. In my mind, I feared he would categorize the "pain years" by these emotional tirades. He didn't. Years later when I mustered the courage to ask Bill's perspective on my anguished flare-ups he recalled, "It seemed like you would go for months and months trying to make sure your pain affected us as little as possible. We had some intense conversations over the four years but I only remember three or four melt downs in that time. I saw them as points where you couldn't cope like you usually did because it became too much to bear. It was like you just couldn't control it anymore."

He was partly right. But I do recall using some self-control by choosing not to attack *him* with my words, not to swear or routinely throw things, all of which I certainly felt like doing at times. Pain has crazy-making qualities.

And while complicated emotions followed these kinds of scenes, this one in particular had an upside. I let God, my husband and myself know that I still had some fight in me. And, thankfully, the glasses were only the cheap reading variety.

* * *

It's tempting to complain when living in chronic pain but it doesn't help. In fact, as Marva Dawn explains in *Being Well When We're Ill*, it can make matters worse. "To whine about our woes merely focuses our attention on them and, it seems, actually increases our pain because we become so conscious of it."

I certainly had my moments of ranting when the emotional exhaustion of mucking through the mire of pain overtook. And, God used the writings of a fellow sufferer to challenge my approach and call me to living well in the midst. Dawn writes:

Our choice is to concentrate on our language, so that we discipline ourselves simply to report our pain, rather than gripe about it. Informing other persons about our pangs is usually necessary so that they don't touch us where we hurt, hug us too tightly, or make noise that will increase our headache. But we can do that in a way that only asks them to take proper precautions to prevent further injury and does not request prolonged conversation that will intensify our attention to the pain. (pg. 123)

I found freedom in this admonition as it resonated with a deep concern that I could become nothing more than my physical issues. The idea repulsed me.

Silence became my go-to coping mechanism. Because the source of my agony happened to also be the vessel of spoken words I often opted to shut it. Bill endured many evenings with little conversation as I struggled to be present, kind and survive until bedtime. Watching sports together became our shared activity, letting commentators fill our living room with talk. I wasn't much fun but he didn't complain, nor did he fill his world with involvements that took him away. I'm sure he could have found many reasons to be with others who were far more engaging but he didn't. He just hung out with me. For years.

* * *

Harrison Lake—July 23, 2012, I wrote:

The clouds sit low and heavy over the mountains, blurring the line between lake and sky. Grey. It's all so very grey. The lone orange buoy lilts and sways with the gentle waves. The waters are calm while the rain dots the surface, leaving pock marks of interrupted peace.

Two loons are out for breakfast. I join their morning as they pause at the end of the dock. They look at each other, one dives, the other disappears and I must lean forward from my chair to find their point of resurface. They are surprisingly close as they come up. One head turns to meet the other's eyes and they repeat the routine again and again, all over the lake. Seemingly oblivious to the rain, the lake provides their nourishment.

I am not so unaffected by the weather. The grey. The heavy. The weight of the morning rests on me. And yet there is a peace and simplicity to this. So little is expected of me when the sky says "stay indoors." There is no call to paddle or hike or explore or even move outdoors. Just sit. Feel the heater blowing on my legs and thank God I'm not tenting!

Here at the lake, it's just a different day. The pressure of needing sunshine is gone, largely, I suspect because there aren't three little boys here to be entertained indoors all day. That season is over. It's quiet. Not a lot of boats on such a dreary day. And peaceful.

Is this picture of the lake akin to my new life? There is a certain dull, uneventful quality to it. The foggy blurring of the scenery reminds me of the undefined time this is. I don't have a clear view of what's across the lake. Yesterday, a different season of life, the mountains were crisp, trees evident, sun danced on water and radiated light and life. Today it's hazy. Vague, distant outlines remind of the presence of other but with little clarity. But I know what is across that lake because I have seen and I remember and I know that simply because the clouds descended, nothing has really changed. Nothing that really matters has changed.

It's called dead reckoning, I believe. As sailors of old or kayakers of now set a course based on visual landmarks, I set my course years ago. The compass—adjusted to the seen—becomes the guiding force in the time of unseen. Don't change the settings. The readings are trustworthy and when all visual contact is lost in thick fog, press on. Trust that what was, is. Who was, is.

* * *

Two days later, I wrote:

Today it was two herons that flew by as I sat with my tea and laptop, drinking in the gentle ripples of the morning lake. Yesterday, my hummingbird zipped in, enjoyed the scarlet verbena, feet away from mine, and just as quickly darted off. We had a racoon visit as well. He scooted down the patio stairs to water's edge, sat on his haunches and washed his face and hands.

I kayaked yesterday. The afternoon waters were the most still I've ever seen here. We paddled slowly and carefully down the shoreline, an anchored sailboat as my dead reckoning goal. It wasn't effortless but certainly a stroll on the lake. And I was powering the boat! I kayaked!

As I stroked the waters toward the sailboat, it occurred to me that the very conditions we deemed ideal had paralyzed the sailor. His boat remained anchored in the cove, no winds to power his movement.

So what are ideal conditions? I keep returning to a friend's thought that because of our sinful nature, we want to possess. I might come to this place and wish it were mine—start calculating and figuring, "how could we own such a spot?" In that posture, I miss the moment, it seems to me. If I'm focused on owning, I'm not focused on God, on the people I'm with, on the beauty in the moment.

I think I have learned something about this, materially speaking. I can come here and give thanks for means to rent and just enjoy this beauty. I can be grateful that some-one else is willing to do the work of creating and maintain-ing and I can just partake. Even with kayaking, I see this. I don't long to own the boat anymore. A simple afternoon paddle on a pristine lake satisfies me. It may be the only paddle I do this year, but honestly, it's more than I dreamed I would do!

So if I'm understanding—at least catching glimpses of—what it means to relinquish a desire to possess earthly goods, can I do the same with my life? Do I want to possess my life? It feels like an odd question that flies in the face of boundaries and ownership, where we are encouraged to take up our own lives and protect the treasures within. What does it mean to lay down my life? What is it to fully surrender? If my purpose is to glorify God and enjoy His presence, what does that look like today?

There is really nothing I have control of. If I'm honest, as terrifying a thought as it is, I control or possess noth-ing. News this week of people killed in a landslide—eating breakfast one minute—gone the next. A young man de-cides to swim across a river, can't make it and a family is plunged into despair and sent down a path of who knows what. He's alive, but how damaged? How will he now glorify God and enjoy His presence?

My life is not my own. God, what do you want for me? I have given up work and while it was hard to do initially, I'm not missing it. It doesn't feel like much of a sacrifice, rather more a relief.

If my life is not my own, any breath I take, any difference I make in someone else's life is a gift. I deserve nothing—worse than that, really. I am not entitled to health or a suffering-free existence. I own nothing and am owed nothing. In that spirit, how then shall I live?

How to live indeed. Manage pain. Reduce activity. Wait. Wait for the day I see the Minnesota surgeon and pray that the cost and energy expended in traveling east will produce answers. I hope.

* * *

From Minnesota, on August 22, 2012, I wrote:

Dear family and friends,

As I sit here in a hotel room in Minneapolis, my head spins with all that has happened in the last few days. I will try to capture a few of the important pieces and not bore you with too many details. Please do know that God has protected, intervened and provided in very meaningful ways. Thank you for praying.

I discovered on Friday that the surgeon I met with is part of an elite, international association of TMJ surgeons, only 28 in the world. It is amazing to me to reflect on God's leading to this point as I had no idea such a "club" existed. My case will be presented to the international community for input and I am being referred to a surgeon in Toronto. Yes, there's a Canadian member!

My hope for this trip was that I would leave with more direction, answers and a plan. While I hardly know where to begin in capturing it, I do have a plan. The short version is that we must determine if my limited range of motion is structural—if there was no pain, would the joint even open? I have a series of techniques that I must now work on to see if mobility can increase. Please pray as they are very painful to do. The next step would be sedation and having the joint forced open to its widest extent, tearing off tissues. Apparently recovery is long and miserable but the procedure can work, if the joint isn't constrained structurally, which leads to another possibility.

Parallel to this, we are further investigating the removal of the implants. The good news is that I will likely not require total joint replacement. The plates could be taken out, bones scraped clean and nothing else would need to be inserted. This track has a life of its own, has more questions than answers and is the reason for the international discussion forum. These TMJ specialists, who research extensively in this field, have never heard of this type of implant nor do they know what they are made of. That's another whole story.

Indeed it was a story unto itself. The surgeon looked at me as if I had two heads. "It can't possibly be made out of titanium. They weren't using that material in 1980. At least I've never heard of it being used that early."

I replied, "Well, that's what I've been told by the original surgeon, although he wasn't 100% positive."

"And you say you only had glenoid fossa implants? Why do you have four scars?" he asked.

I reiterated my account of how the surgery was performed: neck incisions used to insert wires for dislocating the jaw and cuts in front of my ears for the implant procedure. He balked, "You don't need four incisions for that surgery. Are you sure you don't have condylar prostheses as well?"

The penny dropped. I had traveled all the way from BC again and he had not looked at the scan results from my visit two months prior. Anger, frustration and the fear that I had wasted money to be here swirled. I wanted to sarcastically ask 'do you think I had this done in a Phoenix back alley?' I tried to be gracious. "I'm pretty sure the scan confirms what I remember."

"I want to do another panoramic x-ray. Can you come back in on Monday?" Thankfully, I could and did. "I'm going to refer you to my buddy in Toronto. There are only two surgeons in Canada who do this and David is the most conservative of the two. I'll send him a letter with my findings."

As you may gather, this is not straightforward and there is no simple answer. All options initially lead to increased pain with the hopes that eventually there can be decreased pain and greater joint mobility. It feels both encouraging and daunting. I am constantly being reminded that I only have to live this moment and trust the Lord for all the moments to come. God continues to give evidence of

His presence and provision over and over again and I am grateful.

Thank you again for your prayers, emails and encouragement. I fly home this afternoon—another leg of this unexpected and never dull life-journey behind me.

With love and appreciation,

Shelaine

* * *

September 2, 2012, I wrote:

If I truly believe that God is sovereign, then how does that change the way I live today? Practically speaking, where does the belief in a sovereign God intersect with my daily life? When the paperwork that was supposedly sent from Minnesota to Toronto hasn't arrived three weeks later, my human reaction is, "Are you kidding me? Three weeks wasted when I could have been on the waiting list!" Disappointment, frustration, and fear all seem reasonable and understandable, given the circumstances. But to stay there—to live from that place—seems counter to the belief that God is sovereign. It seems that to truly live from belief is to step back and ask, "Where are you in this, Lord?" or, "What are you seeing that I'm not?" or perhaps it can even be, "How do you want me to respond to this news?" Other possibilities come to mind, thanks to Marva Dawn's writing. "Where are the glimpses of the Trinity? Where do I see you, Lord?" I could be asking, "What do you have for me in this time of waiting?" and maybe need to even consider, "What are you protecting me from by this delay?"

The thought that lingers with me is that rarely do these questions get answered quickly, clearly or directly. Sometimes I am blessed with a glimmer of insight in the moment that helps give clarity and builds my faith. But more often I simply have more questions and am led back on the faith-loop to the place of asking, "Do I believe that God is sovereign? Am I willing to believe that His ways are higher than mine and if so, what difference will that make to me today?"

One answer I do have is that my anxiety is reduced, my planning and pursuing takes a rest and I enter into the present moment more. Choosing to not research endlessly, pursue every option relentlessly, and live today, brings rest. I guess it is an act of trust to release my efforts and believe that God is making something happen. The faith-gap lies in what I don't know He is making happen. I must choose daily to sit in the space of uncertainty, believing that my pain is not wasted, my quiet is not lost on Him, my days are not without purpose. I just don't get to know right now.

What I do know is that I am regularly given the grace of gratitude. God is redeeming my vision so I can see people, creation, and moments with a clarity and appreciation like never before. What really matters? A plan followed through or a deep connection made? The dishes washed quickly or a hummingbird studied as it stared back through the kitchen window at me? Will I take up the opportunities presented to me today and embrace them; not treat brief encounters with others as insignificant or inconvenient? Will I adopt a God-view and see each moment as a gift, each breath as an extension of my life, each event as part of a watched-over, orchestrated and eternally important scene in God's plan? Will I choose today to rest on the wings of the One who swoops under and carries His young like the eagle? Would someone watching me today step back and say, "She must know a sovereign God. I can tell by the way she lives."

*   *   *

September 18, 2012, I wrote:

Two weeks ago today, Clark left for school and I felt like that would mark the beginning of a time to rest. Two weeks ago today, the denial of my disability application arrived. As I reflect on the coming together of those two events, it felt like a double blow to me. I believe I was looking to the fall months as a time to quit. The previous six months of being off work were revealing to me just how much I need- ed to be done. The two sessions I did over those months showed the price tag attached to teaching. The cost felt too high. I began to accept that and to admit that pulling out completely would be best. I would accept the time as a gift where I could justify not doing, not earning, just quitting. I was finally able to free myself to admit that I needed a break and to take it. I believe that was possible, at least in part, because I had applied for disability and was told that it would be four months before a decision would be made. In a sense, I was working toward having an income, albeit passively. I was blindsided by the denial letter arriving less than one month after my application was complete.

The letter came as such a shock. I had begun to believe that I would be eligible. All the voices around me telling me how much I should qualify were convincing. I felt lulled into a place of waiting and expecting that this would be God's provision for our family. That I could rest and be "taken care of" while the government did its work simply did not happen. Not even for one day.

Instead, I was moved into another doctor's appointment, more decisions, more advocating, more—not less, not quitting—more tracking down of information, more phone calls, more internal distress. Do I really need disability? What if I do all this work and still don't qualify? What does God ask of me in this time?

And now I sit on the other side of all those questions and phone calls and letters and decisions. I'm thrust back into the place of waiting. I have decided to appeal the decision and my doctor and wise counsel seem to think I have a strong case. There is a sense of exhilaration in taking up the challenge of the appeal.

And then, periodically, I have this flash of reality. My goal has been to convince the powers that be that I am disabled. By definition, I have a medical problem that is both severe and prolonged and will prevent me from work in the foreseeable future. That's what I'm pushing to be labeled. Disabled. Worthy of a pension and benefits as one who can't work.

Sometimes I sit back and can't even believe it's me. Sometimes I reflect on Marva Dawn's perspective that to chase after meaning—in other words, to keep pursuing the "why"—is to miss the opportunity to chase after God

Himself. The meaning for this time won't be found in answers to why but rather in God Himself. Her call is that we, the infirmed, look for glimpses of the Trinity in every situation, every moment.

There are so many gifts in this season. The time and energy I have to attend to my boys would make the top of the list. To have been here yesterday for the brief Taylor sighting and to hear a snapshot of his journey felt meaningful. The interaction lasted maybe four minutes. I was home, mid-day, for this fleeting interaction, because I am disabled.

Weekly, I have time to sit with Clark and drink tea and talk about life and school and new perspectives. I see the hand of God on this young man's life, shaping him and using his challenges for good in the future. How can I do anything but thank God for the gift of time to walk with Clark in this season?

I am auditing a class that I've wanted to take for years. Auditing. I am thankful.

*   *   *

October 1, 2012, I wrote:

"She is a fighter and tried to cope at work till March 2012 when I advised her to go on Medical EI."

My doctor wrote those words on my application for Disability Pension. I smiled at the part where he "advised me to go on Medical EI." My recollection was that I asked for that. Never mind, that's not the point. And, it's likely more meaningful to the powers-that-be if it was the doctor's idea.

What really struck me was my response to the first phrase, "She is a fighter." Initially, I felt great satisfaction. Something struck a responsive chord within me. That's who I am! I'm the fighter. I won't quit. I will bounce back. I will push through. I am resilient. The statement sat as a medal of honor around my neck. I am a fighter.

And then I sat with it longer. What's behind that? Is pride lurking and keeping me from full surrender and submission to God's best? Where does my identity as fighter really move out of healthy resilience and zest for life to stoic independence and unwillingness to need?

This is such a curious time. I draw upon the fighter-girl to take up the appeal with disability, put my best grace-fight forward and then find myself astounded that this is my life. I step back and look at what I am fighting for and can't believe that it has all come to this. I am vigorously pursuing a label I have spent a lifetime avoiding. The irony is shocking. Fight to get to quit. That's what it feels like right now.

There is a longing to be taken care of somewhere at the heart of all this. The disability pension feels like a permission to quit, like a validation that all the pushing through can cease. The pension would relieve some of the pressure around not contributing financially to our family. It would be a small cushion to ease the on-the-edge-ness of our finances during this time. It could let me off the hook. That's really the issue. Bill is so very supportive of me being off work. I am the one who does the books and sees the realities and feels the absence of my contributions more starkly. I carry the overly responsible first-born traits.

And there is growth. Perhaps another gift that comes out of pain and loss. News of a financial reversal didn't rock my world for more than a few minutes. Then I was reminded that this whole season—funny, it should be our whole lives—but this season bears more characteristics of living from a faith-for-finances place. In the past, our faith has been in giving consistently and sharing from our abundance. Now, faith is for more basic provisions—and even as I type that, I scoff at how I define basic. We have so much. Somehow the larger bills, the ones that I can't scrimp and move from account to account to cover, become the pictures of our utter dependence on the grace and generosity of God. I am growing in faith in the God who provides.

So how can I be taken care of? What do I need, to know that I am taken care of? It feels difficult and yet so simple at times. My needs are met. My rest comes in my ability to trust that the sovereign God loves me, accepts me and none of this surprises Him. And yet in my human state, there is a deep-brain longing to be nurtured by human hands and hearts. To hear the words of someone saying, "quit, rest, it's taken care of, be free, relax, nothing is expected of you, stop fighting."

I know that most of those words could be spoken and be meaningless to me unless I receive them. I must internalize rest and quitting and ceasing the fight. So I go back to the comments by my doctor. "I advised her to…" He takes ownership of telling me to stop.

I see that I want it all! I want to be the one who persists and fights the good fight and runs the race with endurance and I also want to be the one who rests on the wings of the

One who carries me. This is not a simple journey. I am not clear cut and simple in my needs. I want to fight. I want to be told to rest. I want to be taken care of. I want to quit.

* * *

On October 9, 2012, I wrote:

Surgically Pressured—should I send this to two close friends?

Dearest friends,

Thank you so much for all the ways you love and care for me. I can't imagine walking through this season of life without the depth of friendships I have. God truly has blessed me over and over and I want you to know how thankful I am for each of you.

Since I have recently had similar conversations with each of you, I decided to write to you both. Hope you don't mind.

As I have shared some of my journey with you, both of you have asked—in one way or another—why I'm not willing to go to MN and have surgery. Why would I even consider waiting a year? In those moments I feel like I have stammered and stumbled and my answers have felt ridiculous and unconvincing. So, here's my best attempt to give you a glimpse into my thinking.

An easy answer would be cost. However, since you have both offered to make finances a non-issue through fund-raising, I find that I can't hide behind that reason. The reality of your financial offer has forced me to consider what really is going on for me. For lack of anything better, all I can tell you is that I am scared.

When I agree to have surgery, I am signing up for drastically increased pain and exceptionally hard work to recover from the procedure. That in itself gives me pause to wonder if I will ever feel ready to take it on.

But the issue is bigger than that. What I live with now is not pleasant or easy, but at least it's a known. There are no guarantees that surgery will leave me in a better place than I am now. There is even the possibility of being worse off. That terrifies me. So when I say yes to surgery, I have to be settled in my spirit that I am deciding to—and prepared to—live with the outcome, whatever it is. I know, that I know, that I know, that I can't feel pushed or pressured into doing it a minute before I can embrace that uncertainty and walk out the consequences of the choice. I am frighteningly clear that while I can have amazing support, I must be the one to live in, through and with this decision.

I have full confidence that neither of you intend to pressure nor push me into anything. I believe that your questions come from compassion and for a desire to see me suffer less. And because I believe that to be true, I want to be honest about where I'm at. Right now, those "why wouldn't you?" questions feel like a judgement—that I'm doing this wrong or being stubborn or I'm ungrateful for the financial offer of help. I recognize that these are my own issues and sensitivities and I wish it weren't so. However, there it is.

It also raises anxiety in me to think that I am wearing you out. I do know that I am not able to enter into your life in the ways of old. I can't play as much, laugh as much, give as much or be who I used to be. I know that you want me to get better soon for my sake and I think there could be a sense of for your sake, too. I believe you miss the old me. I also wonder if the current me isn't a little too needy and taxing. And if that's the case, I can see you wishing that I'd hurry up and have the surgery and quit being so demanding.

I never sent the letter. But the process of writing it clarified my feelings and helped me rehearse how and what I needed to say. I initiated face-to-face conversations with each friend and came away heard and respected. Such gifts.

* * *

October 11, 2012, I wrote:

Our brains are like a spotlight. When we are focused on one aspect, we can't give attention to other things. If that's the case, when I choose gratitude, I can't be envious. This is what I learned in my brain and behavior class yesterday.

The thought takes me many places. If I am fixed on the vibrant fall colors in our yard and I thank God for the beauty of the moment, I am not focused anxiously on the days ahead.

Gratitude requires attention. I can't be grateful for things I zip by or dash past or fly over. I must open my eyes to see differently—to have vision that doesn't skim but rather pauses, hovers, dwells on, soaks in. I need eyes that absorb the moment and take in the scent, the sounds, the textures.

When I focus on life with a lens of gratitude all I have becomes sharpened. My lack blurs to the outer edges. With a thankful heart I am rich and see abundance. Without it, I crave, want, envy, and seek after. And when I lose the grateful perspective, I lose. I miss the small gifts that come to me every day in the most unexpected ways or means.

Without attention to the gift of the present, I forget about my walk through the neighborhood, feeling desolate and longing for a friend. I lose sight of the quick prayer, asking God for Himself revealed with skin on. I miss that He provided the friend, seconds after that prayer, getting out of her van. She had time for a hug and a quick visit. That's all. But a heart of gratitude took the gift and multiplied it into a day-changer. God gives good gifts.

If I am not grateful, I feel hard-done-by. I look at the bank account dwindling, the Master Card to be paid and I must choose. Will I give thanks for a lifetime of faithful care and provisions? Or will I anxiously try to sort it out in my own strength. Thankfully, I mostly choose thanks. I make a deliberate choice to acknowledge that the One who has provided, will. I also choose to release my expectations for how that will look. I am learning that God is sovereign and that if I believe that, it must change the way I live every minute of every day.

Gratitude moves me away from entitlement and my heart is humbled when I choose it. I am not owed so everything I receive is a gift. Repeatedly we see how God goes before us and makes a way. How much do I miss because I'm so busy taking care of things? God's way, the way of gratitude, is above and beyond anything we could ask for or imagine.

* * *

The misalignment of my degenerating joints played havoc with my entire body. The left side continued to lose muscle mass and strength leaving me susceptible to injury. It also created a difficult dynamic as pain sapped energy while managing whole-body discomfort required I not sit or stay in one position for long. My solution? I walked. Not up mountains or down steep grades, but the thousands of steps I took each day kept me sane.

My route was predictable—once around a small lake not far from our home. On a good day I might be able to go twice. At another stage of life I would have deemed the same trail boring and ventured more widely. But this worked and I found variety in the little things like who joined me and even where we met. One park, five entrances, and five standing dates with girlfriends. I met Rosabelle at the mall parking lot, Cheryl by the dock, Sue at the workout area, Lisa by the ball diamond and Karen by the playground. I walked with other friends as well but those meeting spots had to overlap with my regulars. I could handle that degree of change.

* * *

Friendship and chronic pain are a curious dance, resulting in toes being stepped on when it's necessary to alter how things used to be for sake of survival. Grief was real on both sides of relationships as I had to pull back, missing out on the joy of input from important people. My friends expressed a similar sense of loss since I could not be as actively involved in their worlds. We all had our lives to live and sometimes the two paths no longer crossed.

November 7, 2012, I read Matthew 26:36-46:

> Then Jesus went with his disciples to a place called Gethsemane, and he said to them, "Sit here while I go over there and pray." He took Peter and the two sons of Zebedee along with him, and he began to be sorrowful and troubled. Then he said to them, "My soul is overwhelmed with sorrow to the point of death. Stay here and keep watch with me."
>
> Going a little farther, he fell with his face to the ground and prayed, "My Father, if it is possible, may this cup be taken from me. Yet not as I will, but as you will."
>
> Then he returned to his disciples and found them sleeping. "Couldn't you men keep watch with me for one hour?" he asked Peter. "Watch and pray so that you will not fall into temptation. The spirit is willing, but the flesh is weak."
>
> He went away a second time and prayed, "My Father, if it is not possible for this cup to be taken away unless I drink it, may your will be done."
>
> When he came back, he again found them sleeping, because their eyes were heavy. So he left them and went away once more and prayed the third time, saying the same thing.
>
> Then he returned to the disciples and said to them, "Are you still sleeping and resting? Look, the hour has come, and the Son of Man is delivered into the hands of sinners. Rise! Let us go! Here comes my betrayer!"

And then I wrote:

> I wonder about the tone Jesus used when asking his disci-
> ples these questions. Was it disappointment that His friends
> couldn't bear even the smallest piece of His burden? Was
> it judgment on three who failed a test of faithfulness and
> support? Was it teaching that given all their best intentions
> and thoughts of themselves, they would come up short? Or
> was it simply a statement of fact that while they might have
> wanted to support Him, they were too weak? As humans
> we fail. Even our best intentions fall short.

> This is likely the place in the story that I feel the most
> sense of connection. I have shared my pain and need for
> prayer with the larger circle of friends and asked them to
> walk with me through this time. They are at a further dis-
> tance and largely keep informed only as I send email up-
> dates. They rarely enter in beyond that point.

> Then there are a few friends with whom I have shared
> more of the agony of this journey and have asked them to
> walk more closely with me.

> But what do I do when those with whom I have shared
> and been most vulnerable, "fall asleep?"

> One commentator says, "It is well for us that our sal-
> vation is in the hand of One who neither slumbers nor
> sleeps." Jesus knows what it is to walk the path of suffering
> alone. He shares my heart's longing for companionship
> and someone to share the burden, share the journey. He
> knows that people can't do it. They will fall short of my
> desires because they must be walking their "alone" path
> while I'm walking mine. There will be times when I can
> call them to action, give specific requests for prayer. But I

must come to terms with this being a solitary journey into the center of the garden. There is a point beyond which no human can accompany me. There was a point where Jesus knew to ask His friends to stay behind—that He had to do this most agonizing suffering alone with the Father.

The cry of my human heart is for love with skin on and arms around. And, my soul knows that it needs love from the only One who can truly identify, always hold me, perfectly walk with me and fully understand me. Oh God, may I learn to lean into you more and onto humans less.

* * *

As lonely as some of those pain-wracked days were, my friends were faithful and continued to show up, as best they could. November 2, 2012, I wrote:

The other night, when Rosabelle came over for tea, she commented that my house is a very restful place. Joey arrived yesterday and fell into a chair, leaving the world of care for her Alzheimers-ridden mother behind. Is this my vocation, Lord? For this season, am I to open my fireplace to those who are harried, exhausted, burdened by the life that goes on outside my door?

I wrestle with this curious place of feeling, at times, like I just want someone to take care of me. And I want them to do it without me having to ask for it. Spontaneous acts of care. The challenge arises when, just as quickly, I love being able to minister to someone and be the "doing-for" person.

Rosabelle and I chatted the other night about my being off work. I reflected afterwards on how little time in my life I have not worked. Starting with babysitting at a young age, there have been only a few short spans where I haven't earned income. And, when I wasn't earning, I was volunteering.

One space where I didn't work was in the months leading up to my wedding. I arrived in Manitoba to live with mom and dad, completely exhausted from my work as Community Life Intern. I didn't apply for Employment Insurance because I wasn't trying to find work. The combination did not go well with my dad and the messages that it is not okay to not work were further drilled in. It went deeper than that. Being completely worn out and emotionally depleted was not a good enough reason to take time off and recover. Self-care, it was clear, was really a combination of two four-letter words.

So what have I learned, as a child, as a young adult, as a middle aged+ woman, about work and self-care and myself? Is it legitimate to take time out of my prime years of earning potential and sit? In these days of waiting for a decision from Disability, I find myself so conflicted. I truly want to be free of all commitments that resemble work. When I can just quit and be home and have no activities on the horizon, I am better. There are enough stuff of life things that fill my calendar that those extra days drain me when I actually have to perform professionally. I am more aware of anxiety within me when I book things. Sometimes I wake up in the morning with a tightness in my muscles that only relaxes when I remember that little is expected of me in that day.

But if I can invite the Joeys and Rosabelles of the world into my sanctuary and listen and interact with them, can I coach? Is it reasonable to think that I could add an hour or two of my week, dedicated to doing a similar activity, and get paid for it? Or does the pressure to perform and the anxiety of the preparation and the contract expectations to fulfill defeat the purpose of time off? What is this time supposed to be, anyway? I will not rest fully until some of this pain is addressed. And will surgery be the answer? Hard to know. So this time is about giving the most oppor-tunity to not spiral down into physical exhaustion—adding work and stress to high pain—and to maintaining my emo-tional wellbeing.

In many ways, sorting out the physical wellbeing is fairly straight forward. I know that if I speak to a group, I pay for it two to three days, at least. If I get exercise and move throughout my day, I fare better than if I'm sitting for long periods. Being home is less tiring than being out. Physical-ly, it seems like the perfect day would be to stay home and walk laps around my house.

Emotionally, I can't see that going well. I need purpose and I need people. It just depends on the day, and at this stage of life more than ever before, the time of the month. I'm wondering about the wisdom of pursuing some coach-ing work. There was so little thought or prayer that went into that. It's been very much a "take the next step and see what happens" approach. I believe there is merit to that.

But if I really believed that it is okay for me to fully step out of earning right now, would I have even taken one step? Is this about not feeling I have permission to fully quit? Or, is this about keeping purpose and people in my life in small, manageable ways while I crawl through this season of pain?

The other piece that astounds me is that it's November. I have been off work at Strategic for seven months and I don't miss it. Is that possible? Or was I so ready to be done with that portion of my life that I can close that door and move on? In all honesty, I haven't really fully not worked. I had the summer mostly off from paid work but by the end of August I had a contract. Then there was one in September. And October had both paid and volunteer commitments. I didn't earn much, but there was always something on the calendar.

I suppose there is no simple answer and probably no right answer either. I try to hold this time and space with an open hand. I don't want to waste the time given. I believe it's a gift to have these days of relative freedom and open-endedness. I want to embrace what I am being given and also be able to look back at this time with confidence that they were days well spent. Not because so much was accomplished, but rather because they were in keeping with God's best and His priorities. Be still and know that I am God.

* * *

Eighteen days later a letter arrived from the Disability Pension Plan announcing my approval for monthly benefits and the additional unexpected news that each of our sons would receive money as full time students, and we would all be issued back-pay to my July application date. December 10th our bank account jumped as the promised money arrived—an amount just slightly larger than the outstanding balance on our line of credit—debt we had incurred from the Minnesota trips and appointments. We were being taken care of. I had been given permission to quit.

*   *   *

Eating continued to be a challenge as my mouth had not regained any more range of motion, meaning I could only open 19 mm or three quarters of an inch. While I did have capacity for up and down chewing action, I could not tolerate biting down on anything that gave resistance. On many occasions a tough piece of carrot hidden in a seemingly safe soup reduced me to tears.

We were now empty-nesters for the eight months our sons were away at university, so my cooking demands, and food costs, were greatly reduced. God had provided a way for me to be off work that allowed for endless hours of "free" time each day. I also felt convicted that while my choice of food was greatly restricted, I hardly suffered. I knew that the bounty of variety available to me still far exceeded the daily nutritional options for much of the world's population. To fill with self-pity felt wrong. A two-pronged philosophy toward food grew.

My bottom line became *I eat to live, I don't live to eat.* This was particularly helpful on special occasions where I often had to pass on 90% of the offerings. I learned to snack before we went out or take something jaw-friendly along. I never went hungry and endeavored to give thanks that I could participate at all.

The other approach to food came out of my growing recognition of the daily sacrifices and acts of support from my husband. Bill never—and I do mean never—complained if dinner wasn't ready. In fact, there were many days he would come home and cook. He also maintained a positive and grateful spirit about whatever version of mushy vegetables I set before him. I desired to make meals that didn't always look or taste handicapped.

One particular event solidified my commitment to creating tasty meals. The women's ministry group at our church planned a retreat at a local camp. As I filled out the registration form I encountered the section titled *Special Dietary Requirements*. I zipped past it, assuming I'd just cope and find options on the buffet, and then stopped. If they were asking, why wouldn't I say that I am on a soft food only diet? So, I did. And promptly forgot about the comment.

A couple weeks before the event I received a call from the camp. The woman asked for information on my diet and instructed me to go to a particular table at each meal where I would find a plate prepared for me. I doubt she will ever know how touched I felt to be so specifically cared for in the midst of a large group.

Sure enough, a meal with my name on it was hot and ready for every dining experience. I was so grateful and sat down to enjoy the food with other women at a table. At one point over a dinner, a woman across the table commented, "I didn't realize that soft food meant bland food." I hadn't noticed.

But the thought stuck with me and became an impetus for research. I dove into seasonings and new recipes. Several times a week I tried something different and Bill and I enjoyed flavor bursts like never before as I spiced food more aggressively. Only later did I learn that jaw issues can dull one's sense of taste. Thankfully, Bill has an eclectic palette and strong sense of culinary adventure.

And, I missed salad. Of all the foods stricken from my diet, the absence of crunchy fresh vegetables, a mix of greens, fruit and dressing left the largest void. I particularly wanted Greek and spinach salad and set out to customize them for my jaw.

I diced tomatoes, onion, zucchini, peppers, and Kalamata olives, tossed them in olive oil and seasonings and baked them in the oven. Once cooled I added small pieces of feta cheese along with Greek dressing and enjoyed my salad. It's true, there was no crunch but the flavors satisfied.

Cooked spinach took a little longer to adjust to, but I was committed and persisted in steaming the leaves, cooling them and topping them with mashed strawberries, goat cheese, cashews crushed to powder and sesame dressing. Taste isn't a replacement for texture in food but I chose to be thankful that I had time and resources to make nutritious meals fun and with variety. In fact, the restrictions of my diet moved me to the healthiest and most nutritionally balanced season of eating ever.

* * *

The start of 2013 marked the beginning of a new era, namely writing beyond my journal and letters.

Bill's work as a university professor affords him a break from the teaching routine every seven years. In anticipation of his upcoming sabbatical, he sought an opportunity to teach one short course in Phoenix and give me a reprieve from the wet, cold BC winter. I found accommodations for the month and we set our sights on being snowbirds. At the last minute, the class was cancelled, and in faith that finances would permit, we went anyway.

Our Christmas gift to our sons was a road trip to Phoenix with their dad. I flew, knowing that such a long drive would inflict a miserable toll. My left shoulder, which had been deemed 'frozen' in October of 2011, had responded minimally to bi-weekly physio and was scheduled for an MRI in February. I knew that 20+ hours sitting in a car would exacerbate that issue and, also, my left hip. My imbalanced, misaligned jaw was wreaking havoc on my entire body, particularly the left side.

We all arrived in Arizona via our different means and I shared the "This is your life, Shelaine" tour with our boys. For the first time they saw the house I lived in, the jaw story baseball diamond, and the desert I so love. We enjoyed our days and then sent the young men back to BC to carry on with university while Bill and I settled into our sabbatical life.

About two months before we left for Phoenix I had panicked. How would I spend hour after hour in a city far away from friends and any routine for pain management that I had developed? I contacted one of Bill's colleagues and inquired about her non-fiction writing course, noting that I would be out of the country for the first month. She offered to allow me to audit the course—but do all the work, just no deadline or grades pressure—and participate from Arizona for January. With fear and trembling, I registered.

Bill entered Phoenix task-minded with his book revision project and I knew I would need to put in time to meet the demands of my course. We agreed to spend mornings writing, afternoons exploring and evenings relaxing. Bill wrote in the living room. We bought a folding table for me and set it up in the master bedroom, in front of the sliding glass windows that overlooked the man-made lake in the center of our condo complex. In the early days I wondered how I would ever fill the time sitting at my station and writing. About what?

I decided to start with my recent experience crossing the border to catch my Arizona bound flight.

The overhead sign informs me that the approximate wait time in Sumas is five minutes. My schedule has some wiggle room, but I still take a breath and feel grateful that the line will be short and I'll soon be on my way to the Seattle Airport.

Traffic flow agrees with what I know to be true of short border waits. I round the curve, no cars, cross the tracks, no slow down and pull up near the Duty Free parking area. There are likely 20 cars in my lane and maybe ten in the one beside me but it appears only one wicket is open. I muse at how the five minute estimate will be slightly off as I anticipate two lanes merging into one. Fifteen minutes. Or maybe they will open another crossing window.

Out comes a guard, a hopeful indicator of progress or, wait, no. Seriously? Our one lane now has a big orange cone in it, stopping all traffic, while Guard 1 speaks to Guard 2. It's a brief interruption in going nowhere quickly and we're back in business. Until, minutes later, the scene repeats itself. And then again. And yet again.

Thirty minutes into my estimated five-minute wait, I recognize that I have travelled approximately two cars lengths. I am pretty sure my typically low blood pressure, isn't. Now all of the mergers have done so and we creep ahead. One car in front of me now. The long awaited green light flashes on and slowly he proceeds. I breathe a thankful sigh, reach down for my passport and look up to see the car stop half way to the hut. The guard is marching out with his in-your-face hand fully in stop mode, and he places the cone back in the lane.

I'm doing the math now. It's normally three hours, without traffic issues, to the Seattle airport from here. I left myself five hours for the whole trip knowing that I ought to arrive two hours ahead of the flight. I have now spent one fifth of my leisurely morning traveling 200 feet. I review the extra transition time I will need with dropping the car off at Park 'N Jet and taking the shuttle to the terminal. I negotiate and rearrange the plan mentally. I must get gas, that one seems important. Bathroom break just became a luxury I couldn't afford. Eating is overrated and besides, somewhere in one of my suitcases is a protein bar. That will do.

I wonder if Mr. Guard knows the stress he's causing. As the brake lights of my in-front-of-me friend release and I get the green, I make a mental note not to share my "I'm trying to catch a flight" story. I have a sense he doesn't care. And, I have a bigger sense that it might just slow him down.

I've now been preparing for my turn at the border wicket for almost 60 minutes and yet as I pull forward, I'm flustered and fumbling with my passport. I don't usually drive this particular car and I seem to have missed the "Oh, by the way, the driver's window doesn't really roll down any more" memo. With no hands on the steering wheel, two hands on the window crank, I squeak out a three inch gap that I can barely slip my passport-holding-hand out of.

"Is your window broken?" the guard asks with a slight snarl. Not really the start I was hoping for.

"Yes, apparently it is," I reply with a smile. I sensed this wasn't the start he was after either.

As he scans my official document that reveals all my innermost secrets and information, I continue to wrestle with the window and succeed in gaining two more inches. He doesn't seem impressed with my effort.

"Where are you going?" he asked, never looking away from the screen. "Seattle airport to fly to Phoenix," I reply, pleased that I have offered only accurate, not excessive, information.

"How long are you going for?" Again, no eye contact. "One month," I answer. Now he's looking at me.

"That's a long time. Who are you meeting there?" he probes as he scans the monitor.

"My husband and three sons."

"Where are they now?"

"Oh, somewhere between Las Vegas and the Grand Canyon," I reply lightly. Clearly not sharing the excitement of their chance for adventure, he asks, "How long have they been in the States?"

"Since Thursday," I answer, watching his eyes rapidly dart back and forth across his secret files on the Strom family.

"What kind of work do you do?"

"I'm a career counsellor but I'm currently on a medical leave." Now I'm really on my game, answering concisely.

"When were you last in Arizona?" Did he just say Arizona? I'm pressing my ear through the available 5 inches of open window but feel I should clarify, just in case he really said the States.

"Arizona?" I ask.

"Yesss," he hisses, "that IS where you are going, right?" It was hard to miss his sarcasm.

"Yes, I was last there in April, the beginning of April." I'm pretty sure he was just really enjoying our time by now so he went further to ask, "How long were you there?"

"About a week." Can we be done now, I begin to wonder? Best not ask.

"When did you last work?" I'm beginning to wonder if his computer is broken and he's now updating records. "End of March," I reply.

"Where does your husband work?" Feeling confident and slightly excessive by now I offer, "He's a professor at Trinity Western University." Surely his voracious appetite for seemingly unrelated information must be nearly satisfied. "How long is he staying?" Once again, I reply with, "A month."

He feigns genuine shock, "He's off work for a whole month?" As soon as I respond that Bill is on a sabbatical, I regret it. His brow narrows and he glares at me. "So he's working?"

"No, he's on a sabbatical leave from his work." Argh, there's that word again.

"So then when did he finish work?" Now I'm getting full-on wordy and explain that he works on a semester system so he was done before Christmas when he finished marking exams and his sabbatical officially begins January 1st. When will I learn? "So he IS working now?"

"No," I concede, fully defeated, "he is on holidays." I'm pretty sure the look from under his eyebrows meant, 'Why didn't you just say that in the first place?' Who is on first, anyway?

I'm feeling pretty confident now that I'm not a risk to national security and that we've established who is and isn't working when and where. Can I please go and try to catch my plane now, I mentally plead with him?

"Turn the car off and pop the trunk. What are you taking with you?"

"Clothing and…" Clearly I'm not taking exciting enough things.

"Fruits or vegetables?"

"No," and then he's gone to the back of the car, sorting through my bags.

Oh. No! He's not opening anything. I locked my two check-on bags and I put the keys…somewhere. I grab my purse and try to discreetly feel around for them. I check my pockets, attempting to not look guilty. No keys. After all, it was 6:30 am when I locked those bags. Where are they? At this point, I surrender mentally. He wins. I decide that I'll just raise my hands, turn myself in and admit that yes, I had a plane to catch and no, I won't ever do that again.

I envision being hauled into the "area" and while they are stripping the car apart, using gigantic metal cutters to open my teeny little travel locks, I will be calling the airline, begging for mercy and a rebooked flight. Problem. I'll likely not be allowed to use my cell phone in the designated "wait here while we destroy your car" zone. Maybe I'll try smoke signals. Back to reality, oh my, but how will I explain that bag of frozen salmon in my suitcase?

And with that jarring thought, Guard-man is back. "Don't lock your suitcases when you are crossing the border!" he admonishes. He holds out my passport, far enough away that I must squeeze my bicep out the window slat to grab it. "Okay," I manage to squeak out. I don't bother to thank him or wish him a good day. I'm pretty sure he feels better already.

I attained speeds of 140 kilometers per hour and made my plane with four minutes to spare.

* * *

The writing course gave some direction, my vision began to change, and writing prompts appeared everywhere. A walk around the little lake blossomed into a narrative on the local birds, their personalities and roles. I wrote:

Something dramatic in goose world broke. I awoke to squawking, screeching and honking at levels nearing hysteria. Two of the birds sat on the complex wall and swore violently at passing cars, innocent pedestrians and the universe in general. And not just for a minute or two. These birds tore strips off the world for half an hour and then, with no apparent resolve, dropped to the outside of the fence and ate grass. I'm pretty sure my geese need therapy.

The condo itself, complete with its idiosyncrasies, provided content for a piece on how comfortable we become with our surroundings.

I've heard our adult children refer to issues of this nature as first world problems and that list would be topped admirably by the satellite dish that cuts in and out without warning or apparent cause. Managed from its home base in Edmonton, we wait to watch our favorite teams at the mercy of refreshing rates and distant analysis. Whim Satellite teases us with enough performance to hope that we might see that big game on Sunday. And while we are powerless to affect change, we are not without regular updates on the system's status—Satellite Acquiring Signal—and then politely requests that we Please Wait. Oh right, it's Canadian.

Each day I eagerly made my way to my computer and found the morning hours zipping by. Often Bill would be standing at the end of the hall, shoes on, keys in hand waiting for me to finish "just one more thought." My mind whirled with ideas and momentum grew.

But no one was reading any of my words. The distance from the face-to-face of the classroom provided a necessary anonymity as I worked up the courage to put my work out for scrutiny. I started by emailing each new piece from the bedroom to the living room, asking my husband to read them as I hid ten feet away feeling vulnerable and exposed. At first I asked that he just read them and say if he liked the idea or not. Then I dared request a few comments. As confidence and belief in my abilities grew I sought his eye for critical review. I had long been an editor of his work but now we had a together-activity, something we call 'mutual edit-fication.'

One of my biggest hurdles was the mental shift from "I am a speaker/teacher/instructor/facilitator" to "I am a writer." I love story telling as a means of making lessons livelier and points more personal but I had only done that verbally. My writing had previously been a place of private emotional processing. I struggled to find my voice as I continued to note events and encounters like this mall experience:

> I was searching for my men. Our cell phones were functioning with hit and miss regularity as they adjusted to Phoenix. I was tense, alone and walking briskly by store after store, scanning over the sales racks for my family.
>
> Mid-stride my path was blocked by an extended arm offering me a tattered, well-used square green envelope. My eyes darted directly to the body and face attached to the mystery hand to find what my dear old grandmother would have called a shady character. I was in the presence of a stereotypical drug dealer. I was being offered the goods. Years of media training had taught me well and the phrase came effortlessly. "Oh, no thank you." That's the slogan, right? Just say "No thank you" to drugs. Perhaps spoken words aren't always as accessible as I like to think they are.

The gift of Phoenix was an established morning writing routine and growing passion to do so. I had no idea all God intended for my newfound love.

* * *

After returning to BC, I continued to spend my spring writing. The course challenged me to see the world as a prompt and five or six days a week I sat at my table—the same one we bought in Phoenix—now set up to look onto our backyard. I used the location as opportunity to challenge my skills by crafting a piece on how our ivy had changed over the years. By the time the edits were done I realized I had written not just about plants but about our growing and transforming family.

Auditing a course never involved so much participation as I began drawing on my vocational past to fuel stories for class. I picked particularly poignant memories of clients like the one who scooped me up and began carrying me out of the room during a small west coast earthquake or the woman who pooped on a chair mid-session. More and more faces and tales came to mind marking the birth of a manuscript eventually titled *Changing Course: Stories to Navigate Career and Life Transitions*. (Available at: http://www.shelainestrom.com/changing-course.html)

The career project grew as I developed a template for the stories and recounted crazy and meaningful experiences in the classroom with people in transition. I worked diligently, not for the sake of being published, but rather to do the work I knew God had for me in this season. Little did I know the healing power the exercise would have as words to page brought emotional closure to my lengthy run with Strategic and the career development world. Another gift.

* * *

Gifts, by nature, are often unexpected and the most cherished are ones that connect to our highest values. I treasure this letter from our oldest son.

February 19, 2013

I'm reading Evangelium Vitae (the Gospel of Life) by the Late Pope John Paul II. Its primary focus is abortion and euthanasia, however, I found a quote that made me think of you, and I thought I would share it as a way to encourage you.

"Living to the Lord also means recognizing that suffering, while still an evil and a trial in itself, can always become a source of good. It becomes such if it is experienced for love and with love through sharing, by God's gracious gift and one's own personal and free choice, in the suffering of Christ Crucified. In this way, the person who lives his suffering in the Lord grows more fully conformed to him and more closely associated with his redemptive work on behalf of the Church and humanity."

I see, in you through this time of trial and tribulation, the image of Christ Crucified. That is, the love you have shared with me and others, regardless of your suffering, is the love of Christ. I don't have much wisdom, nor experience, but I think that your suffering with your jaw has been and is a source of good. I would never say that the pain and all that comes with it is a good thing, but what has come of it is remarkable. So, please take it the right way when I say that your suffering has been a blessing to me.

I pray for healing for you, so don't get me wrong, I don't relish the idea of you staying in pain one bit. I just think it is important to recognize the closeness to Christ that has become ever-more evident through this time. Thank you for choosing to suffer with Christ Crucified, and by doing so, drawing yourself, and me closer into God's redemptive work.

Love,

Taylor

* * *

If ever there was a contrast between my daily living and an event I participated in, it came in the form of 11:07.

Throughout their years at Trinity Western University, all three of our sons were regular players in the comedy improv show 11:07, held every other Friday night. The start time matched the event name—11:07 p.m. That in itself should have determined my availability given my strict 10 p.m. bedtime routine.

Over supper one night, our sons asked Bill if he would like to join their team for our oldest's farewell show. One son offered, "Mom, you can be in it, too. We just didn't think you would be able to. It's so late and laughing causes you so much pain."

Can I afford the energy expense? What muscles will hurt? How long will recovery take if I say yes to this request? Will it damage me or temporarily increase existing pain?

Can I afford not to? Is this something that's time sensitive —a once in a lifetime opportunity? Is it relationally valuable, far beyond the price of energy or physical demand?

Sometimes the answer simply had to be, "Yes, I'll do that."

The fact that I had never done comedy improv didn't cross my mind. My kids were inviting me into something they valued greatly in a season where I too often felt I had to say no. We had long been team Strom and now we were about to hit the stage.

The frenzy the event stirred on campus shocked us all. We knew our sons had become a legend of sorts on the improv stage, feeding off their long-worked-on brotherly humor and zany antics, but the excitement that built over the Strom parents playing felt over the top. My husband, Dr. Strom the communication professor, was about to assume a very different role and students loved it. My recent endeavor into the classroom and encounters with students in our home earned me a pre-show fan club. It was one of those moments as a parent when we realized the Strom brothers' stage reputation was giving us a few seconds of local fame. It was delightful.

The theatre was packed with standing room only. Our opening skit met expectations as the crowd howled with laughter and fed us with applause. By the end of the night Bill and I decided that we weren't going to give up our day jobs to do comedy professionally but felt proud that we hadn't embarrassed our kids either. Little did we know the future significance comedy improv would have in our lives.

And the price I paid for that night was high. I crashed into bed after 2:00 am, my body rebelling. I slept fitfully, unable to find any position comfortable enough to allow me more than a few minutes of rest. Pillows propping me up. Pillows flat. Pillows between my knees, under my arms, around my neck. Ice packs. Heat. Voltaren. Tylenol. Advil. Morning came slowly and the escalated pain didn't relent. Nor did it for the following three days as I secreted away from the world trying to regain my old normal, hoping I hadn't permanently upped the intensity.

Slowly the crisis levels reduced and I could, once again, bask in the joy of the family memory made. Yes, the cost was worth it. I just longed to have one without the other.

* * *

Over two decades earlier Bill and I scanned through the Yellow Pages looking for a church that resembled the one we had been attending through our dating months. Now married, we desired connection with a local body, not the one-hour commute each way we had been driving to a service. Perhaps there are more spiritual approaches to discerning God's plan but He seemed to honor our feeble method. We've been members of the same church since 1988.

As is true with all congregations, there have been storms to weather and we've seen much change during our time at Ross Road Community Church. We've also developed some lasting relationships, our children had a safe and loving community to grow up in, we've had leadership opportunities and a place to serve. Overall, church is a place I've wanted to be.

But pain changes things. Everything, really.

Each Sunday morning we arrived at church right as the service began so I could avoid chatting in the lobby. We took our place in the second or third row and I took a deep breath as the worship time began. I didn't sing. But it wasn't like the days of old when I thought I couldn't sing.

Many times I told my clients the story of being a nine-year-old, first-born, over-achieving perfectionist who wanted to please everyone and disappoint no one. When my music teacher said "play the xylophone," I played; when she said "shake the tambourine," the bells rang out; when she said "sing," I sang. Until.

Until the day I read my report card. "Shelaine is a lovely young girl but she can't carry a tune." The message was clear. I couldn't sing and I didn't for over a decade.

In university a roommate asked me one day, "How come I never hear you sing?"

"Because I can't," I replied matter-of-factly.

"You may not be a rock star, but you can speak so surely you can sing. Why don't you try?"

Back and forth we went until I stubbornly decided to illustrate my point and prove her wrong. No hum-a-tune-in-the-shower or join-in-with-the-radio-artist for me. I tried out for the university choir. Unfortunately, I made it.

I enjoyed the choir experience enough but learned more about me than I did about music. For over ten years I had let those few words of another person define how I viewed myself. After the school term ended I didn't return to the music department, not because I felt I couldn't sing but rather because I decided I didn't like it enough to carry on.

For years following the university awakening I enjoyed singing in church and came to value that weekly expression of worship. My new choice to be silent was pragmatic and sad. Each time I opened my mouth the muscles surrounding my jaw tensed and began to spasm. I simply couldn't afford the luxury of singing.

And then there were the instruments. Each crash of the cymbal sent a lightning bolt through my jaw and out my temple, particularly on the left side. Vocalists hitting high notes and guitar solos that moved up the scale sent my left hand over my ear and side of my face in desperate attempts to minimize the intensity of discomfort. Only much later did I learn how many people were aware of my church survival behavior.

"Is my singing that bad?" the woman to my left leaned over and whispered with a twinkle.

"No," I replied, "the cymbal is hard on me. Covering my ear and jaw helps a little." Note to self—explain coping methods to new seatmates.

On several occasions I stood wondering why I was there. *God this is so painful. I'm so distracted by my own pain I can't focus on You anyway. Should I just stay home?* One memorable morning I recall asking similar questions and the phrase came to mind, sacrifice of praise. I felt struck. *Is that what You want this time to be, God? Is being here enough? Can it be that enduring the pain of music is my spiritual act of worship?*

I approached each Sunday service with a new perspective. I saw the silence of my lips as opportunity to hear the lyrics. I closed my eyes and let the words wash over me, drawing attention away from myself and more to God. Many of those mornings held rich and deeply meaningful moments.

But it didn't take away the challenge of the church foyer. Being part of a community where people care is an incredible gift. I know that strangers and friends faithfully upheld me in prayer and God used their acts of kindness on numerous occasions to encourage and sustain us through those wilderness years. And, they wanted to know how I was doing, often approaching me after the service and inquiring in the loud, people-filled lobby. Most well-meaning people simply did not put together that talking about a sore jaw made it sorer and projecting my voice to be heard in such a busy environment hurt.

Emotionally, I desired people's care and interest and I didn't want to talk about it, creating an ongoing internal battle. The struggle with feeling like I was seen as no more than my jaw problem was at its highest in the foyer. And many days I just avoided the interactions by bolting out the sanctuary's side door with the final amen.

* * *

I would not have gone from career coaching to writing had it not been for my health issues. My husband was the writer, not me. But God opened that door as I sought Him and ways to find meaning and purpose in the midst.

Periodically I felt my motivation for the career project lagging and I'd need a new writing challenge. Why not try my hand at another type of writing, I thought, resulting in this article called *Waiting: A Passionate Pause* which was published on the Truth Media website. God had much larger designs for it than I could have imagined.

At age 12 years and 11 months our middle son, Clark, made known his request.

"Mom, I will be 13 soon and I'd really like a hamster for my birthday." Then he waited silently, head tilted slightly, eyebrows peaked, brown eyes begging. "They're so cute, Mom."

As the voice in my head screamed, "There will be no rodents living in my house!" I heard myself gently reply, "I'll talk to your dad," and hoped this would be another passing phase.

A week or so later, Clark found me in the laundry room and took up his case. "Mom, I was thinking about getting a hamster. Here's the thing. I would have to take care of him and that would teach me to be responsible."

My internal resolve quivered. "And," he continued in all seriousness, "being responsible will help me be a better parent someday to your grandchildren."

We picked up a hamster on Clark's 13th birthday.

Jimmy, of the Teddy Bear hamster variety, shed new light on the meaning of routine. Nocturnal by nature, he spent his days sleeping and his nights running and running and running as if the whole world was on fire. His cardiovascular fitness remained unparalleled.

Periodically, however, Jimmy would halt abruptly and stiffen. Head shifting to the side, eyes peering, he considered something beyond his wheel. Then, just as predictably, he resumed pace and raced his way to morning.

Almost daily, Clark plucked Jimmy out of his world and placed him in "the Globe"—a clear, plastic ball. And without fail, each time his feet hit the plastic, Jimmy assumed his motionless statue posture. Immersed in new circumstances, Jimmy remained frozen until his little muscles could bear the tension no longer. A leg twitched and the ball responded. Another small body movement met with a corresponding shift to the orbit, and before long, Jimmy raced around chairs, under tables and past stairs—blocked off for his preservation.

Observing Jimmy and his repetitive schedule—sleep, wake, eat, run, repeat—reminded me of people I knew. In fact, while hesitant to admit it, I am a lot like Jimmy the hamster. For years I entered my wheel of family life and work, be it paid or volunteer, set my eyes forward and ran full tilt. Every so often I glanced left or right, wondered if different awaited me, and just as quickly got back on pace. Venturing out would be scary, but more than that, the security of sameness kept me going.

In addition to being married and raising three sons, I worked as a Career Coach and Instructor for over 17 years with the same company. While new people entered our job transition program each month, I taught the same course, in the same schedule and with my trusted co-workers.

And then news came that our program lost funding and we would be closing our doors in six months.

At the same time I was enduring ever-increasing pain from a long-ago jaw injury. Teaching required projected speaking which only aggravated my discomfort. I pressed on, propelled by loyalty to team, love of my work and a desire to finish well. I also had an end in sight.

A little over a year ago, my work concluded, my pain kept soaring and I received word that the surgery I require is at least another year down the road. Fully removed from my hamster wheel, I entered my own plastic globe.

A lot like Jimmy, my first response looked like paralysis. Exhausted and afraid, I grieved the loss of the life I once knew. And God said, "Wait." Months passed and as I rested, my muscles twitched and my orbit moved slightly, ever so slightly. And I began to see that waiting is not what I once thought it was. As Sue Monk Kidd says in her book, *When the Heart Waits*, "One day, while I was reading in the Gospels, it occurred to me that when important times of transition came for Jesus, he entered enclosures of waiting—the wilderness, a garden, the tomb. Jesus' life was a balanced rhythm of waiting on God and expressing the fruits of that waiting."

Waiting in the presence of God during initial stages of change is tough. To believe that there will, in fact, be fruit from waiting requires faith. Daily I must choose to believe that I am not forgotten—I'm not set on a shelf without greater purpose. I am held in the hands of the One who knows who I was, who I am and who I am becoming.

Sitting in this sphere of loss and waiting can feel pointless—like a waste of time—but is it? Sue Monk Kidd continues, "I had tended to view waiting as mere passivity. When I looked it up in my dictionary however, I found that the words passive and passion come from the same Latin root, pati, which means 'to endure'. Waiting is thus both passive and passionate…It means struggling with the vision of who we really are in God and molding the courage to live that vision."

Catching a vision of how God sees me is both quiet and dynamic. My activities are restricted and reined in by pain, pulling me out of the mainstream and stilling me. And yet during these seemingly inactive times God actively challenges my false beliefs. My true-self-awareness grows as I ask, "How do you see me, Lord?" He gently responds, "I am sufficient for all your needs. Wait in me." And slowly I begin to grasp who I am, not just what I do.

It's likely safe to say that Jimmy did not know my son's intent when transported from cage to globe. I do not know the why behind the change and pain I live in. At first Jimmy had no idea that relocation meant new worlds opening up because the loss of safe sameness feels raw, empty and frightening. But much like the critter who caught a vision to explore, I too am finding new ways to understand myself and see life through God's eyes as I wait.

* * *

When the boys were young I wanted to be the "neighborhood mom," the one whose front door stood wide open welcoming all the street's kids to drop in for hot baked cookies and a glass of milk. I wasn't. Those busy times with three sons in three and a half years stretched me to the edge of energy and I pushed hard simply to keep up with them. Extras were rarely a doable option.

But God knew my heart and gifted me with that long wished-for role during my season of unemployment. It began with one young man who needed a place to stay for a few days and developed into our youth hostel service, providing room and board for several young adults in transition between school and summer work or longer. My husband and I agreed that we wouldn't charge them to stay with us as an expression of thanks to God for all the ways He was meeting our needs. Ironically, our own children informed their friends of our long-standing family policy: If you can't find a summer job, you volunteer somewhere or work for us around the house. It had proven to be a great motivator for our own sons to find paid work and grew into an enormous help in a season where my husband had to add many of my normal responsibilities—like cleaning and grocery shopping—to his already full workload.

In those weeks of early spring we had three to five young men painting our shed, re-coating our deck, cutting the lawn, weeding flower beds, power washing the house and even digging a ditch around the foundation so drainage tiles could be replaced. The exchange of meals and a bed in a family environment for help around our property satisfied all parties and laid the foundation for lasting relationship with our "extra kids."

* * *

On August 4, 2013, I wrote:

This is my life.

When my work ended—partly due to a contract drawing to a close—and largely to release me to a place of easier pain management, I entered into what I called a "waiting room." Friends labeled this time for me in many ways ranging from a palatable "season of waiting" to the more difficult to embrace "being set on a shelf." The words used to capture this experience of pain varied but the underlying sentiment remained consistent. I am waiting.

As these months became a year and then more I find myself asking if waiting is truly what I'm doing. I regularly have people commenting on how patient I appear to be as the months roll by with no further medical appointments set. How can I stand having to wait so long? Why am I not phoning to see where I am on the waitlist? Those questions are not quickly or easily answered but here's my best attempt at the short version.

I'm too busy living to be upset about the waiting. Somewhere in this process a shift has occurred for me. Yes, it is true that my name appears on two lists in the office of two separate surgeons in two other provinces. I have come to believe that perhaps that's where the idea of this being a season of waiting needs to end.

I have no job waiting for my return should this jaw issue be resolved. Any work I do from here forward will be different from what I have done and will need to be fashioned to fit my current life circumstances, which, of note, is very much what I'm doing right now. Granted, my capacity to earn is minimal as pain and energy restrictions dictate but I participate in meaningful work-like involvements every day, as they fit with my current life circumstances. Hmm.

If I look at this life-season from a values perspective, I am hard pressed to think of a time that fits better with what I care about most. I am largely available to spend time with my adult sons—according to their schedules—because mine is so flexible and fluid. And my husband of over a quarter century and I are having more laughter, shared time together and relaxed interactions than we've had in years. Pain is stress but a great reduction in outside stressors affords us opportunity to explore newly found shared interests in writing and discuss how we might successfully kayak together.

Waiting, I'm coming to believe, implies relying on future circumstances to change in such a way that life will be better or happier or more comfortable. I do believe that my life will not look like it does today ten years from now. What I don't want is to find myself somewhere down the road looking back and saying, "What a waste. I had all that time and I missed living those days." No, I purpose to live each day as a gift with a mindset of living, not waiting. I want to ask God where He is in this day, in this moment and then be fully alive to the joy, the pain, the laughter, the sadness—whatever the day holds.

* * *

"Go to the purple wall, turn left and follow the signs. Take these papers, sit in the hallway chair and the technician will come and explain how to fill out the forms."

Within minutes of finding my way to the appropriate waiting area, Janice appeared and beckoned me through the door ominously covered with warnings and restrictions. Thankful not to be struck dead upon entering, I willingly sat where told. Janice delivered her well-rehearsed speech with warm precision.

"Go into that room and remove all of your clothing, except your underwear. All jewelry must come off. Put on the very big brown pants and blue gown, opening to the back. Bring all your belongings out to this locker and bring only the key into The Room. Fill out the paperwork and I'll be back to review it with you." As she turned to walk away, I ventured, "I am wearing a pain patch. Does that need to come off?"

"Yes," she replied emphatically, wide-eyes punctuating her words, "and you must thoroughly wash the area to remove any traces of metal that might be on your skin." She turned again, leaving through an unmarked door.

I followed her instructions precisely and returned to lock up my possessions, all in one hand so the other could keep the pants from falling to my ankles...again.

Janice returned before I could read all the labels on the massive meat-locker door. *STOP! Danger, Restricted Access! Strong Magnetic Field! Magnet is Always On!* I would so not want to work here.

Picking up my clipboard, Janice reviewed my answers, most of which came easily.

Yes or No, do you have:

Vascular stent—No.

Wire mesh—No.

Penile insert—No.

Bullets, BBs, or shrapnel—No, pretty sure I'd remember if I did.

Claustrophobic—No problem there.

Metal plates, screws, artificial joints—Yes.

Janice's eyes met mine. "Your jaw, right?"

"Yes, but that won't be affected, will it?"

"It shouldn't be a problem. Just last week I had a patient with facial bones fully reconstructed in titanium and he was fine." I smile, aware that her left eye twitched slightly when she said he "was fine."

"Well, it's not clear if my plates and screws are titanium or stainless steel. Is that going to be a problem?" She must have sensed my anxiety as her tone softened and she began speech number two, the one designed for people about to scream and run wildly from the room, dressed of course in the gown opening to the back and pants sized for giants. "Everyone has different sensitivity levels and, if at any point you feel uncomfortable or experience pain, just squeeze the button I'll give you and we'll stop immediately. Then we'll sort out what we have to do from there. I'm sure it will all be fine." More fine.

With that, Janice opened the vault and out came a woman who appeared to have lived through the experience. She is informed that she moved quite a bit early in the test but hopefully the latter images will be sufficient. Note to self. She may have to come back. Movement is bad. Be completely still. I am not repeating this affair.

The inner sanctum looked a lot like other imaging rooms I have frequented. I was handed earplugs and asked if I knew how loud the machine is. No, I really don't, so she quoted stats on jackhammer-level volume and laws requiring ear protection during scanning. I tucked the yellow hearing preservers in my ears as I climbed onto the table, careful to align body parts exactly as instructed. After a few tucks and tweaks, she placed the "I'm freaking out" bulb in my right hand and told me to feel free to squeeze it if I needed out.

I assume she pushed a button and my table began sliding into the tube. Expecting it to be a brief trip, I closed my eyes and waited and waited and waited some more while the table kept moving, sucking me deeply into a black and very small tube. I felt very far in. Eyes scrunched tightly, my overwhelming urge was to squeeze and eject immediately. But I had waited four months for this MRI and I wasn't going to miss the chance.

Shoulder? Don't care anymore. Just want out of here. Want to be anywhere else. One little pulse on that bulb. No, I must be perfectly still. Even my breathing cannot move my shoulders.

Breathing. Now there's a thought. Filling out the form in the waiting room, I breezed through the question on claustrophobia with an air of arrogance—No, that's not me, I'm not claustrophobic. If that's the case, why can't I get air into my lungs and why does it feel like the elephant these pants were designed for is sitting on my chest? Get a grip, girl!

Open your eyes and see what's happening. I did and was surprised to find my tube-of-perceived-dark-confinement had two bright strips of light above me, leading right out to my feet, which were protruding in the open air. The realization did not immediately bring oxygen to my lungs. I willed myself to breathe in through my nose, out through my mouth, as I recalled directives from Mental Health First Aid on guiding people through panic attacks. And in and out. And again.

My debate raged and competed with breathing strategies 101. *I could squirm out on my own, if I had to. I have a panic button (let's be honest and call it what it really is) if I really need to stop. But I want to have this scan. Lie perfectly still. Motionless panic and I'll be fine. Breathe. Breathe.*

I can't say whether the self-talk did it or I simply find comfort in ear-splitting blasts. Whatever the case, my breathing eased when the monster roared to life and began clanging and banging around my head.

I mused at my stress over the next 20 minutes of utter stillness and excessive racket. I've never been so close to a full blown panic attack. What happened? I recalled Janice's admonition to wash off all residues which might be present from the pain patch, ensuring there were no microscopic metallic remnants left on my skin, which could cause painful burns. However, she assured me, I didn't need to worry about the metal plates and screws that I know are in my jaw! Hmm. Maintaining my immobility, I shifted my eyes to the left. If those plates and screws were going to be sucked out of my head and attach themselves to the side of this magnetic tube, I wanted to see it!

No such excitement. With only an occasional shooting pain, the rattling and shaking ceased and captivity ended. Remembering to hold up my pants, I threw the earplugs in the garbage with the nonchalance of a survivor. Janice offered, "You did great. The images are excellent. You held perfectly still." She was so congratulatory I thought I might get a gold star. No thank you, I reconsidered, that would be metallic.

* * *

The MRI had been for my shoulder. My physiotherapist had recommended the MRI and my doctor had concurred, ordering the test and referring me to an orthopaedic surgeon.

I waited in the surgeon's examination room noting how refreshing it was to have new pictures to look at. No jaw emphasis in here. I studied the shoulder joint, noting how many muscles connected between the head, neck, arm and upper torso.

"Mrs. Strom. I'm Dr. Syal." I exhaled with relief at the warm manner of this young doctor. He proceeded to review the MRI results. "You have damage to your left rotator cuff, a small tear in the labrum and evidence of tissue calcification which tells me your shoulder was frozen, correct?" I affirmed his findings as my thoughts raced. Three and a half years prior, when the hiking incident happened, I believed my jaw to be responsible for everything else hurting so I had pursued relief only from that angle. Only when I couldn't lift my arm over my head or reach back to fasten my bra did I seek help specifically for the shoulder. Thank God for a skilled physiotherapist who mobilized the joint as much as he could while I lived in ignorance to the inner damage of that joint as well.

"….surgery."

The doctor's word brought me back to the moment. "Sorry, what did you say about surgery?" I asked, cringing at the thought.

"Your injury does not warrant surgery, however you are an excellent candidate for an x-ray guided cortisone injection into the left shoulder joint. That should reduce the inflammation and allow you to gain more range of motion which should, in time, reduce your pain."

Sign me up. One less part of my body that screamed day and night would be a gift. The procedure was booked for September 5th and delivered as promised. Thankfully.

* * *

Attitude is a topic I frequently revisited as I endeavored to live above my physical circumstances. I never wanted to become a grumpy old woman and I certainly didn't desire that label at mid-life. The theme kept coming up in my writing and the *MB Herald* published *The Hard Work of Gratitude* in October 2013.

It's so easy to complain.

Last January, as I sat in Phoenix away from the damp B.C. coast, I had an opportunity to rest, read, and write. My husband and I soaked in the beauty of desert life and relished local culture and events. We shared a sabbatical, a luxury not taken for granted.

Yet I recall being aware of the nature that resides within, the part of me that's constantly threatening to turn my head away from the Gift, toward the self.

Unseasonably cold temperatures distracted from the sun-filled, expansive blue skies, and I caught myself grumbling at the need to change clothes three or four times a day. The mornings were cool and required jackets, even mitts. Around noon, I would sit on the deck in full sun, wearing a tank top and shorts, aware that I ought to be careful not to burn. A walk around the lake mid-afternoon proved too chilly for the shorts. Then, evening demanded an ensemble much like early morning.

First world problems, my children would chide.

One night, my husband and I watched comedian Ron James on TV. Our lives aren't too difficult, James said, they're too comfortable. The audience laughed at the irony of the statement, but his words gave me pause. When my world is too comfortable, I dwell on what's missing and forget what I have. Often, a sense of entitlement surfaces.

A few months ago, a friend and I had a conversation about suffering and pain and growth. She told me I had developed the spiritual discipline of gratitude, noting how I continually choose a posture of thankfulness in spite of my physical pain and multiple losses. I thanked her for the kind words, and continued to ponder what she said.

Despite my friend's observation, I'm aware of how ungrateful I often feel. Life is hard, to use a cliché. It's rarely what you expect. And if you hold too tightly to your idea of how life should look, disappointment prevails.

I didn't expect to be unable to work at age 47. Life will let us down. As one of my long-ago clients would say, "Suck it up, buttercup."

But we don't just absorb the disappointment into our psyche and have it disappear into nowhere. Like sponges, we suck up the despair, losses, feeling of being short-changed, and eventually reach a saturation point where we start to drip. Another disappointment hits and becomes like giant hands twisting our sponge, until every drop of inner moisture is squeezed out. And there we sit, crusty, brittle, inflexible, dried up.

Unless.

Unless, by God's grace, we opt for something different. Gratitude, I believe, is a spiritual discipline developed over time, honed in each individual moment when we choose between grumbling and thankfulness.

My sons have recently become intent on developing healthy lifestyles, complete with physical exercise and muscle-building activities. Hearing afresh from them how muscles grow—tiny tissues tear and rebuild, stronger than before—gives me a picture of how gratitude grows.

The example of annoyance at having to change clothes multiple times a day is a "tiny tissue" indeed. However, it represents the subtle way I must choose gratitude in all things, every day. Gratitude is a mindset that grows slowly in the midst of small situations. But it can quickly stop the insidious infiltration of entitlement and discontent in our lives, and open new options.

In my coaching profession, we call it reframing. What's another perspective on this situation? Perhaps by shifting even one degree, life can look quite different. And that's how gratitude becomes a discipline—we willfully move from comfortable whining to a place of thankfulness.

This is not Pollyanna-ish. I'm not fond of the "God is good" reply, complete with cheesy smile and gloss-over approach to adversity. No, I'm advocating an authentic discipline that stares hard into the face of all things difficult and says—in spite of pain, in the midst of suffering, when loss burns to the soul—I give thanks.

* * *

Somewhere over the spring months I decided it was time to tiptoe further into the world of writing and sought a conference to attend. At the encouragement of my professor friend, Loranne—the one whose writing course I completed—I signed up for the Surrey International Writer's Conference.

The registration process produced a cold sweat. Which sessions did I plan to attend? Did I want an individual appointment with an editor, author or agent? And if so, which one and at what time? *Oh grief, what have I gotten myself into?*

The thought of taking a piece of my writing and having it evaluated by an editor felt overwhelming. The idea of pitching why an agent ought to take me on as a client and attempt to publish my manuscript felt ridiculous. I aborted the registration process.

But the call to sign up niggled at me. I reviewed each of the writing professionals and narrowed my choices to only those who wrote or dealt with non-fiction. Then I considered my best times of day—from 9 a.m. until noon—and matched the criteria to the offerings. Only one of the almost 20 agents fit. I signed up and promptly forgot her name.

About a month later my professor-friend came for tea and I riddled her with questions about her writing and publishing experience. We covered miles of ground and she mentioned her agent's name. "What did you say her name is?" I inquired. She repeated the woman's name. "I think she is going to be at the conference. Her name sounds familiar to me." I grabbed my laptop and discovered that not only was she attending, she was the agent I had chosen.

On the morning of my appointment I arrived at the conference feeling queasy, like a poser far out of my element. Send me to a career conference and I could confidently navigate. Drop me into this world of writers and watch me shrink. I felt alone and lost and did the only sensible thing. I retreated to the women's washroom.

After a short meeting with myself and several deep breaths I exited the stall and proceeded to the basins. I turned on the water and looked into the mirror to see the agent standing right beside me. Another big breath. I turned and said, "Hi Carolyn, my name is Shelaine. I will be meeting with you later this morning. In case I forget then, Loranne Brown sends greetings." There, I did it. I networked. I established a connection, my stress level dropped as I could enter the appointment with less unknowns. I walked away confident the encounter had not been a coincidence.

I had never done a literary pitch before and decided that I needed to be authentic about my journey and not try to conform to someone else's formula. My career transition stories manuscript had received positive feedback from my select readers but I lived under no illusion that it would make the New York best seller's list. Writing mattered to me. Publishing, not so much. But I felt called to this process so I sat before Carolyn and tried to use my ten minutes wisely by reading what I had prepared:

"My name is Shelaine Strom and I'm a storyteller.

For the last almost 20 years my venue has been a career transition classroom where I have taught, encouraged and coached almost 2000 adults through job and life changes.

That changed one and a half years ago, however, when a serious jaw condition that requires surgery, ended my ability to instruct. And while the jaw pain has closed my mouth, I have not lost my voice.

I am writing a collection of stories from my work with people who sought direction and tools to navigate the changes they encountered. More often, though, these people simply needed to tell their story. And were there some amazing, bizarre, hilarious and moving stories!

This creative non-fiction book contains my story of transition within my career, growing from insecure facilitator thrown into an unknown field to one who loved á challenging client. It holds within the stories I shared with clients to illustrate points, create connection and assure them they weren't alone. And, of course, it's about the clients themselves and the wild ways they showed up in my classroom.

Career and life transition principles come alive in the dialogue of client interaction and unique circumstances of each character and, I believe will resonate with a North American culture immersed in times of economic uncertainty."

Carolyn was fascinated with my story—the one about my jaw. After several questions about surgery and the injury, I caught on. *She is filling time so she can tell me right at the end that she's not interested in my writing. That's kind of her.*

"How soon can you get a finished first copy to me? I'd like to read the manuscript."

Seriously? I studied her expression to be sure I understood. "Thank you! I can have it to you by December 15th. Is that soon enough?" It was and I did. She had the material in her possession for six weeks and I heard nothing from her.

I wasn't bothered by her silence. Four days after the conference I flew to Ontario for my surgical consult.

* * *

On November 4, 2013, I wrote:

Dear family and friends,

As I waited for the surgeon, Dr. David Psutka, to enter the room, I pondered. How do I adequately explain this circuitous journey to yet another doctor? He entered, greeted me, picked up my chart and said with a smile, "You've really had a circuitous journey, haven't you?" Somehow, I found that oddly comforting.

What followed quickly departed from comforting. He had studied my scans and determined ahead of our meeting that the plates cannot just be removed, as I had previously believed. Both joints have advanced degeneration and cannot be simply "cleaned up." He has put me on the path toward total joint replacement on both sides. So, here's what's ahead.

Plan A is best case scenario. A 3-D CT scan is sent to an engineering company and they construct custom joints, which are put in surgically within the year.

Plan B kicks in if the metal currently in my jaw blurs the CT scan and prevents a custom joint from being created. Surgery goes ahead with the removal of existing plates and compromised bones and an attempt to use a stock joint is made. They often don't fit and, if that's the case, we move to Plan C.

Plan C means the plates are out, the mandibles cut off, acrylic spacers inserted, my mouth is wired shut and I heal for 2-3 months. Another scan is done—now with no metal present—the custom joint is made and I return to Toronto for a second major surgery to have the new joints put in.

As you can imagine, my prayer request is for Plan A. The surgery should be within a year, regardless of which option happens. There are many more details I'll spare you and many things that confirmed God's presence in this journey once again. I am grateful for peace and a confidence that all will be well in the biggest sense, even in the midst of what feels like hard news to me. I will need to be in the Toronto area for a minimum of six weeks when the surgery happens, maybe longer, maybe twice. That feels challenging to me on both emotional and practical levels. I'll miss my family and friends!

As for the immediate, I am very weary and eager for some quiet days at home. Thank you all for continuing to pray and care.

Love,

Shelaine

* * *

Shock. I flew home rattled. I had known I needed surgery but the one I expected was the minimally invasive arthroplasty. Open up the joint, remove the existing plates, clean out osteophytes (bone spurs) and bony ankylosis and stitch me up. Voila. Problem solved. I really didn't think it would be that straightforward but I certainly wasn't prepared for news of bilateral total joint replacement.

Somewhere over the prairies cruising at 30,000 feet the reality began to sink in as I reviewed my scratched notes from the consultation. I learned that I had reached the end of the line. This doctor does the "last resort" surgery and I was his ideal candidate. Patients with zero to three prior operations had the best possibility of a good outcome, meaning an 85% likelihood of decreased pain and a 90% chance of increased mechanical opening. My one previous procedure positioned me well, unlike some of his patients for whom he performed joint invasion number twelve, eighteen or even twenty! And, it is a major surgery with serious risks.

I ran through his comments. *Likely experiencing wear debris reaction causing whole body inflammation. Simply removing the current plates would cause loss of vertical dimension and significant shifting of teeth, creating other issues. Removal of existing plates may compromise the bones. Four incisions, remove coronoid process, surgical braces to immobilize joints, risk of numbness and facial weakness, potential for infection.* Stats and possibilities swirled as I tried to grasp the magnitude of the news.

The new prostheses are made of metal and polyethylene. Have been used for sixteen years. Good success rate but no data on longevity beyond that time. Bring your own funding from BC. What does that mean? And something about subchondral cysts…do I have them or is that a risk with surgery? I can't recall. I won't go to any more appointments alone. It's too hard to capture everything. I need another pair of ears.

The surgeon's smile and warm manner came to mind. He seemed upbeat and optimistic, even a little gleeful. It is, after all, his day job. And, the facts remained. The jaw is one of the most difficult parts of the body to address. Nothing is guaranteed. And I have this adrenal condition that adds another layer of risk. My reality felt complicated and yet I had just said yes to the procedure.

I suppose I knew that I could change my mind and cancel far more easily than the opposite so I had agreed with the surgeon and signed the initial papers. As miles passed and home drew closer I felt in the core of my being that this was God's answer, not just another doctor's opinion. By the time I landed in Abbotsford I knew it was time to begin preparing for surgery sometime within the year.

PART III

The Unexpecteds

"You're fortunate not to have to come to surgery alone. Have a seat in this chair and wait here. Someone will be with you soon." Well, I'm certainly alone now. How is it that I get this cavernous space all to myself? Heated chairs would be a kindness for those of us dressed in hospital gown finery. The nurse called this the recovery room. Why am I in recovery before surgery? I think I should be in the anticipation room.

PACU. That's where I am. Funny name. It sounds like they 'pack you' into this space like sardines. I guess that explains all the beds. That's a good distraction. Count the beds. Ten, eleven, twelve…Each one is strapped tightly with fresh white sheets, brakes in locked position, all poised for those wheeled out of operating rooms today. I wonder who else will be separated by the curtains now slung back, attached to the bleached walls decorated with only blood pressure cuffs and oxygen gear. Empty IV poles stand guard. A tray on wheels topped with a green cloth-wrapped bundle of sterile tools and items sits ready at every station. One of these will be my bed. I hope.

That ticking is relentless. There must be a universal supplier for hospital clocks. Silver rim, white face with black short and long hands, and a blood-red hand that methodically clicks past each black hash mark. I wonder how many accumulated days I have passed staring at these generic timepieces?

Can I be the only person in Mississauga having surgery today? I wish something would happen so I wouldn't hear blood pulsing in my ears. I'm sure my heart beats at other times. I know I am the only one who can undergo this, and I know that I am ultimately not alone. But do I have to wait in isolation again? Is it a good idea to leave patients unattended? I'm cold. I wish I had a blanket. Crossing my arms over my chest isn't warming me but maybe it is holding me together.

Ah, signs of life. I'm guessing they are doctors, not from their street clothes but because they have parked themselves ten feet away from me behind the nursing station. If they've noticed me sitting here at the end of bed four they show no evidence. I feel small but I'm pretty sure I'm still visible. Maybe a solitary woman watching their every move is ordinary for them. One is tucking an x-ray onto a lit screen and pressing close to the hazy gray and white outlines of an anonymous case. "Is that another fracture or a shadow from the positioning for the x-ray?" Back and forth. I'm not familiar with the medical jargon of broken legs.

"Good catch. Let Walter know. How's Jenny?" and with that, I'm on my own. Again.

My feet look ridiculous. The one-size-fits-all disposable shoe-covers splay out as my flip flops scrunch the paper between my toes. From all I understand, these pieces of elasticised blue paper are designed to ensure I track no harmful contaminants from my street shoes into the operating room. I can't figure out the logic of wearing these on the inside of my shoes.

The same nurse who finalized my paperwork, asked my name and birthdate for the fourth time, weighed me and led me away from my family, has apparently done so with another woman. My fellow patient's wheelchair is parked at the foot of bed number one and she stares blankly ahead. She doesn't seem to know I'm here, but then again, neither did the doctors. Maybe she hears my rapid breathing. "Mrs. Randolph," the nurse says too loudly, "you're here for cataract surgery, correct? Let me see your wristband please. You'll be going in soon."

How soon is soon? My operation is scheduled to begin at 8:00 a.m., which is 5:00 a.m. Pacific Standard Time. I have friends gathering at our church to pray for me this morning. It seems a bit over the top but they have a lot invested in this day. We all do.

It's 7:35 a.m. and no one is here for me yet. My stomach is acknowledging my 5:00 a.m. rising and strict admonitions not to eat or drink anything. I stood in the shower, awake before anyone else, reminding myself repeatedly not to slurp any water. In those moments I wondered if it would be my last shower. Ever. It wasn't a worried question, more a reality check. And just in case it wasn't my final cleansing, I shaved my legs.

I didn't need an alarm to be roused into this day but it wasn't a wakeful night either. I suspect some people close to me slept less than I did. It feels harder to be the ones watching sometimes than to be the one going through it. A couple of months ago a friend told me she didn't know anyone more prepared to undergo a major surgery than me. I have done all I know to do to be here and I do feel ready. No. I am eager to get on with this. With hot water pouring over me this morning

I prayed, "God, you have made the path here so clear. I trust you with my life and all the outcomes. Let's do this." That sounds brave now that I think about it. Maybe. Or maybe I just can't imagine carrying on living like I have been.

We started our drive to the hospital by allowing ample time for the lengthy swirl up and out of the condo parkade and any traffic issues we might encounter. It's kind of our two visiting sons, Taylor and Clark, to make this ceremonial trek to the hospital with my husband and me. I didn't want Bill to be alone today and we left our support circle back in BC.

We seemed to be talking in the car but little really registered. I heard but was not listening. I didn't feel anxious in the "I'm paralyzed and freaking out sense" but maybe that is the right term. After all, another definition of anxious is to want to do something very much.

* * *

I'm glad I was required to come to Credit Valley Hospital last week for the battery of pre-operative tests. As Bill, Taylor, Clark and I arrived this morning, the parking lot was familiar. We found a spot in the almost vacant cement slab and headed toward the main building. These men who all hover at six feet or more seemed to have legs of clay. I willed my pace slower to keep back with them. We're not late. Look for the Second Cup, I reminded myself. Seriously, what other health institution uses a coffee shop as its central point of reference for giving direction? "When you arrive on the morning of your procedure, start at Admissions, right across from Second Cup," the nurse had instructed.

The lineup felt surprisingly long for the 6:00 a.m. opening. It seems those of us on the receiving end of this process were more eager to get on with things than the staff. The doors remained locked as I sat in the queue, my husband and sons taking turns in chairs, giving them up as other patients arrive. The Cup opened and the boys headed across the lobby for something to occupy themselves with while I continued my vigilant waiting. At 6:08, staff entered—someone forgot their keys, I overheard—and took their cubical places.

"Shelaine Strom?" Yes, that's me. "Birthdate?" May 15, 1965. "Marital Status?" Married, since 1988 to the same man. "Religion?" I'm a Christian. "Language Preference?" English. "Allergies?" Codeine. "Home Address?" Four provinces away in BC. "How long have you lived at this address?" Since 1990, when we bought our first house. It's where we've raised our three sons and the walls we all call home.

"May I have your wrist please? This is your identification band." All my vital statistics have been reduced to this narrow white strip of plastic-enclosed paper. "And this is for your medication allergy." This one is red, to catch everyone's attention. Alert! Don't give her codeine. Or, like July 19, 1980, she'll gasp for air and feel humiliated as ambulance attendants inject epinephrine, cover her nose and mouth with an oxygen mask and whisk her away from the crowd of on-looking teens at volleyball camp.

"Mrs. Strom?" Yes, I'm listening. "Take these papers up the stairs, down the hall to the pre-op area. Check in with the nurse and wait."

"Okay, guys. It's time. This way." I led. None of us really know how to do this so we cracked jokes about signs and procedures until we found the next stop. Same questions. Same forms. Check the identification band—yes, that's my name. Yes, that's my birthday. Yes, I want to go through with this. I guess I'd rather this interrogation than have the wrong procedure done. Yes, I can put all my belongings in the white plastic bag and put on the blue gown, opening to the back. Yes, we can go across the hall to the pre-operative area and wait. More waiting. Years of waiting.

"It's photo op time," announced my husband. Sure, I can smile squished between my 24- and 22-year-old sons while sporting my white robe, blue gown and matching cloth booties. How else are we supposed to pass these moments? Should we be talking about serious matters? I don't want to. I'm past that now. I prefer the banter and laughter as the boys design a YouTube show called ManChild where an adult sporadically slips into child mode. They just might make it a reality but, if not, it's serving its purpose now.

That's my name called. I too eagerly disengaged from the antics and returned to the pre-op area to confirm my name and birthdate. Step on the scales in the middle of this cramped, crowded portal between the bacteria-laden world and the sterile inner sanctum. I guess it doesn't matter who sees how much I weigh today. Soon it will be less.

"Come this way, please." Like well-behaved sheep we four fell into single file. I don't think the office was meant to house all of us. I felt small, stripped of all earthly possessions except my white robe and flip flops, sitting answering the same questions, as three of my four men towered behind me against the sad yellow wall. I wish Eric were here. I wonder how he's doing. Yes, I can say goodbye to my family now. Wait, the nurse didn't tell me to say goodbye. That's too final I guess. I decided a while ago that I wouldn't say goodbye in this moment.

I had imagined it to be different, somehow, more emotional maybe. But I'm not sad or scared. I just want to get on with it.

I hugged Clark and Taylor and whispered my love for each.

"God is with us," said Bill as he held me close.

"He certainly is," I replied. "I love you. I'll see you on the other side."

The nurse put her hand on the small of my back and directed me one way as my family retreated. I glanced back down the long hall just as they turned and headed back toward the Second Cup. Maybe they needed more words, even tears. I had none left to give.

* * *

I wish my legs would stop trembling.

Years ago, fresh university graduate, I sat in the job interview for my social work position and my legs did this. They shook involuntarily as I struggled to maintain composure and answer questions. My anxiety only increased when hands resting on lap resulted in the heavy vibrations setting my whole body in motion. I almost didn't get hired because I couldn't physically manage the stress of the interview so how would I cope with the job, my supervisor had asked.

Breathe. I've learned a thing or two about stress management over these last 25 years. Tighten toes and relax. Tighten calf muscles. Relax. Tighten thighs. Relax. Breathe. Or, I could leave. Do I really want to go through with this? 7:45 and there is still no one here. I can change my mind. Breathe in, breathe out.

Look girl, you've got two choices. You can get up and walk out of here and never do this or you can settle down and trust the outcome to the same God who has so clearly brought you here. What you're not going to do is stir yourself into a panic. So, what's it going to be?

"Well, good morning. How are you today?" asks my surgeon, complete with scrubs and a smile as he motions me to bed seven. "Hop up here and I'll give you a haircut." *You are cutting my hair? He is sniffling and sounds congested. Is he sick and not on top of his game today?*

"How are you this morning?" I dare ask.

"Oh, allergies. Such an annual annoyance. Okay, lie still while I shave you." The razor is buzzing near my forehead, moving slowly behind my ear. He pulls it away and shakes my locks to the floor. "You have a lot of hair!" He seems to be emphasizing that point by tracing the temple-to-ear path several times before continuing down to the nape of my neck. *I am going to look so trendy with this undercut.*

"I'm curious," I begin, "do you get to have lunch today? Eight or nine hours is a long time to go without a break." What I really want to know is *How's your blood sugar? Do your hands start to shake if you don't eat? Can you concentrate with a full bladder? Will the drill slip if...*

"There's a natural break when I switch from one side of your head to the other so I'll step out of the OR for five minutes and have a snack." *I hope it's a protein bar.* My doctor in BC assured me that medical school is a training ground for lack of sleep, improper nutrition and enduring long hours without rests. *I think that information was supposed to comfort me.*

The razor is quiet. "Okay, I'm going to apply glue to your hairline now to make sure the tape I put on sticks." Oh, that's cold and smells like nail-polish-remover-on-steroids. Maybe this is his solution to allergies. How will I ever get this Crazy Glue off my scalp?

A flash of color—certainly not standard issue hospital white gauze—is stretching by my temple. Fingers pulse my forehead as he secures the tape and presses hard to hold it in place. I recognize that sound—the mix of crinkled paper and layers of goo stripping apart. "Are you using duct tape on me?" He chuckles. "Not exactly." I hope it's sterilized.

"Hold still. This will keep the rest of your hair back from the incision sites." And I'm pretty sure it will cut off blood flow to my head, reducing the chance of blood loss. Each circle around my skull presses in, tightening the vice. *I'm not exactly going to be tossing my locks around. Is this necessary? Oh, my head aches already.*

"Wow, you really have a lot of hair! I don't know if I'm going to get it to all fit in here and be out of my way." And if you can't, then what? He's persisting, tucking, winding around and up, over and over. I wish I could see what he's doing. Finally, he's cutting the tape. "You're ready. Let's go." Yes. I am ready.

Oh, that is quite the mound of curls to avoid as I slide off the bed. My surgeon is marching like he's on a mission. I need to pick up my pace to keep up. We're leaving the recovery area. I wonder where he will lead me now. A mirror! Is that me? I'm staring at this reflection of a face wearing an orange traffic pylon, struggling to find me in it. "Seriously?" I ask. "Where is the camera? This is definitely a missed photo op." He's laughing. "No cameras allowed here." Too bad. My sons would love this cone-head look.

We've turned into a room with five or six masked individuals scurrying around, each preparing equipment or readying something. Wait. Have I just walked into surgery? Where's the gurney that wheels me into the theatre? They are introducing themselves, "Hi, I'm Dr. Nelson. I'll be giving your anesthetic." "My name is Sarah." *Hi, I'm another face behind a surgical mask that you'll never recognize later and I'll be busy doing my job, like I do every day, while you're receiving a life altering procedure.* They are all friendly and chatty like we're about to have tea. I wonder what they'll talk about while I'm under.

This can't be the actual operating room. How can this be a sterile environment if I just waltzed in here wearing my outside-world sandals? They must know how dangerous infection would be for me. Is this really where I say goodbye to old joints and welcome new? The walls are so white—void of decoration—in fact, this whole room feels too empty, except of people. A lone cloth-covered rectangle stands poised in the middle.

"Okay, it's time to take off your underwear and flip flops," instructs one pair of eyes. I'm stuffing the last remnants of my outside life into my Patient's Belongings Bag. The name and room number are blank.

"You can climb onto the table now. Be careful. It's narrow." No kidding. I'm 5'4" and top out at 125 pounds and my shoulders touch edge to edge. I guess I'm not likely to roll over. Someone's holding my left hand. "Let's get this IV started. Small poke and a little sting. Here we go." I recognize that initial burn and whoosh of cold into my vein, chilling my feet, my brain.

This must be the room. Surely they won't move me now, but where's all the stainless steel? The overhead light with its penetrating eyes? There's no equipment here? Don't they need a crash cart and a heart monitor with green lines tracking my pulse and respiration? Has TV been misleading me? Maybe hiding saws and drills and screwdrivers is strategic.

My surgeon has a skull in his hand. "This is you." Funny, I don't see my resemblance in the acrylic model void of nose, muscles and identifiable features. "This was made from the CT scan and shows exactly where I'll cut bones and where the prosthetic joints will be placed. And over there on the x-ray, those are my blue prints that show where each screw goes." Screws. I recall how six months ago at my initial consultation he showed me someone else's head in his office. "Will I get purple screws like the ones on your model skull?"

"Yes, but we prefer to call them magenta around here."

Dr. Nelson is back beside me, lifting my left arm and injecting something into the IV port.

"Is the ceiling supposed to be swirling?"

*　*　*

It's dark in here. My eyes don't want to open again. Where am I? Push the lids up. Wait. Thank you, God! I'm alive! I must have survived the surgery. Can't be heaven. Not enough light. Too quiet. This isn't the recovery room. I must be on the ward. There's no one else here. I'm so tired.

"Mrs. Strom. Mrs. Strom." Someone is talking to me. "Mrs. Strom, I'm Kevin, your nurse. How is your pain? Can you tell me on a scale of 1-10?"

Pain. How much pain? I'm too tired to talk so two then three fingers will have to do. That's not much. Is that really all I feel?

"Mrs. Strom. Mrs. Strom. I'm going to give you some more morphine and Gravol. Sorry, what did you say? I didn't understand. Would you like to try and write that for me?"

I'd nod more but I think my head might fall off. It's so heavy. He must have gotten the message. He's handing me paper and a pen and I scratch *my family around?* "No, I haven't seen them but I'm sure they will be here soon."

I asked for them to be here when I woke up. It's okay. I'm alive. They'll come soon. More morphine. So tired.

"Hey, hon, we're here."

I recognize that voice. My husband. Eyes, open so I can see his face. Yes, he's here now. And there's Taylor and Clark. I am alive! I thought so. Now I'm sure. "Itt'ss shho gud to shee you guysh." Oh, that's hard work. I can't move my teeth apart.

"The surgery went really well," Bill started. "Dr. Psutka said everything went as planned. The custom prostheses fit, but your muscles on the right side are weak so you're wired shut. How's your pain on the 1–10?"

The pen and paper. I hope he can read my glasses-less writing. *2–3, hurting a bit earlier. Frozen still.*

I need to know. *Are the wires short term?*

"Yes, the doctor said you'll likely be wired shut for two weeks."

Do I need second surgery?

"No! Everything fit beautifully."

Such great news! I feel like I could fly off this bed and dance around the room. Oh, maybe not. Lifting my head didn't feel so good. My teeth feel weird. I wonder if I can move my jaw at all. *I can feel it 'dislocating'.* That's probably not true but that's the sensation. My face feels foreign. Maybe it's the freezing.

My boys are quiet. They look pensive and uneasy. I want them to know I'm okay.

Taylor—Do you like my sashion fence?

That's better. They are laughing now at my comment. Weeks before surgery as we sat around the dinner table my highly academic and intelligent son had a brain freeze and commented on someone's "sashion fence." It fast became one of those go-to, inside jokes that we now use just for fun. Knowing I'd sport quite the look post-surgery, I made a mental note to try and remember to use the phrase right away to assure everyone I was tracking. I remembered.

They are still laughing. Maybe I don't have brain damage.

"Mom, you have a little curl on top of your head. It's the only hair we can see from under all of your bandages," noted Clark.

I'm smiling. All I want to do is smile, which is good because talking is so hard. I'll write more.

Ears not ringing.

"That's great," my husband who can't seem to stop smiling either exclaimed.

I must draw them a picture of how I looked before surgery. A circle face. Two round eyes. A smile. Now a tall cone on my head. *Before surg. Orange tape.* And a line pointing to the pylon. I feel almost hyper now. So weird. So thankful to be alive.

"That's what you looked like?"

I'm nodding. Oh, that doesn't feel good. Note to self. Don't move head. Oh, something's happening. Where's the pen? *Freezing coming out! Ouch!*

No one is moving. I think I'm going to puke. *Nauseated. Pls tell nurse.* Somebody go and find the nurse! SOON.

More morphine. Thankfully. Sleep again.

Oh no, I'm going to puke. Where's that tube? No one's here. I don't remember my family leaving. Why do these nurses keep leaving me alone? I hate heaving... Done. Sleep.

"Mrs. Strom. Mrs. Strom." Kevin is back.

"How are you feeling? Is the morphine working? How's the nausea?"

I'm about to show you. Where's that tube? Oh, that can't be good for freshly cut bones. I hope my pleading eyes will get him to make the vomiting stop.

"How many times have you vomited?"

Thankfully, I can hold up one hand to answer that.

"Five times? Oh, that's not good. The Gravol mustn't be strong enough. I'll be right back with something else that will help with the nausea. It's the morphine that's making you feel sick."

I know. Just hurry.

* * *

"Good morning, Shelaine." Morning? Night must be over. That's a different voice. Wait. That's my surgeon. Don't go. I want to talk to you. I have so many questions.

"You look great! Let's take a look and see how you are doing. Scrunch your eyebrows for me. Great. Close both eyes and open them. Fantastic. Smile wide. Perfect. Hey, everything works! You're a real trooper, you know."

I think that's a good thing. I'm more relieved to know that my face isn't paralyzed. Thank God. He's still talking but I can't keep up. Something about staying here until Saturday. Get out of bed soon. Catheter out today. Shoot. I like the catheter. First time I haven't had to get up to use the bathroom in the night for years. Dr. Psutka's gone. Was I supposed to remember something?

*　*　*

"Mrs. Strom. Mrs. Strom, I'm going to help you to the bathroom," offered my day nurse.

I really don't want to get out of bed. I'm fine here. I think it would be a bad idea. I'm not ready. I just won't make any movement toward the edge of the bed. Maybe she will leave me alone.

"Mrs. Strom, you need to start walking to reduce the risk of blood clots. You've had major surgery and lying in bed increases your risk. You don't want clots going to your lungs or brain."

Well, since you put it that way. I'm ready to go now.

My husband, who likes to time all of our walks, tells me I took a full minute to cover the twelve feet from bed to bathroom. Felt fast enough to me. Actually more like a grueling marathon. But I didn't faint. That's good. I didn't faint.

* * *

I see a white board at the foot of my bed. *Today is Thursday, May 29, 2014. Your nurse is: Kelly.* I can see something taped underneath the helpful nuggets designed to re-orient me to life. I've caught Bill's attention and point to the object. I'm turning my palms upward and shrugging my shoulders slightly, my attempt at asking, "What's that?" Thankfully we have a history of playing charades and he's catching on. "Those are scissors. They are readily available for when it's time to remove your bandages."

He's a kind man. He left out "in case your tightly bound head swells so much that the straps of gauze under your chin put excess pressure on your throat and constrict your breathing." It's okay, hon. I know that can happen. Remember? It did when I had my first surgery.

* * *

Why is the white board purple? Stop flipping! Eyes, focus. It's not a PowerPoint slide, I know it's fixed to the wall. What's wrong? What's going on? Where's the pen? *Crashing. Cortef! Should be increased with this. Get nurse!* Stop that board! Room going black. Chest heavy. Can't. Hold. On.

"Mrs. Strom. Mrs. Strom. How are you feeling? We've given you a stress dose to help your adrenal system cope with all the pain medications." Good. That's what I need. White board isn't flipping now. Thank you. Thank you.

Yes, that's better. I thought we had established my need for increased doses of the medication. The anesthesiologist was great. She understood adrenal insufficiency and assured us that I would be given ample doses of a drug to counter the anesthetic and carry me through surgery. I don't understand why my dose wasn't kept high to counter the antibiotics, morphine and super-strength Gravol.

My Adrenal Insufficiency, diagnosed in 2006, had been stable and managed effectively with minimal daily doses of Cortef. However, my endocrinologist later confirmed that living in such intense pain stressed my body beyond what the chemical replacement of cortisol could do, rendering me in a low-grade state of adrenal crisis for over three years. The evidence was in a larger crisis that occurred simply by starting antibiotics a few months ago.

In spring of 2014, my doctor excised a suspicious spot on the back of my neck and removed stitches a week later. My medication-thinned skin wasn't fully healed and the incision popped open in the shower the next morning. I opted for a walk-in clinic appointment and was put on antibiotics as the wound looked slightly infected. By the second dose of the Cephalexin my body felt ten times heavier, I could hardly catch my breath and my husband whisked me off to Emergency. The conclusion? Adrenal crisis.

How could I have missed that? I knew to increase my own medication for times when my body was under unusual stress but apparently the extra hadn't been enough. At the time the experience felt miserable but provided much needed insight for surgery.

* * *

My husband is sitting faithfully near the end of my bed to the left, between me and the window looking onto a flower and plant-filled courtyard. The mobile tray table hovers at my immediate left, awkwardly situated given that's my IV hand. Another 'meal' tray sits largely untouched. The menu labeled Wired Jaw Clear Fluid stares at me: *Tea 175 ml, Sugar, Orange Juice 114 ml(2), Vegetable Soup 170 ml, Regular Gingerale 355 ml. NO DRINKING STRAW ON TRAY.* Apparently all caps isn't a strong enough message. The straw sentence is also highlighted in orange. Got it. Sucking is bad for jaw surgery patients.

Eating is awful. Nothing tastes normal. Tea is the most disappointing. It has a metallic flavor that lingers. And the method is awkward. I have a gigantic food syringe with a three-inch red tube attached to the needle end of it. Bill suctions liquid into the body of the unit and then I'm supposed to slide the tube between my cheek and teeth so the fluid can pass beyond my back teeth and down my throat. It's so uncomfortable just getting it in my mouth. The surgical braces holding my teeth together are full of hooks and sharp edges. I have gopher cheeks. There's so little room for anything in my mouth. I need Bill to move the tray. Too much work. No thanks, not hungry now.

I'll sleep.

* * *

Some friends gave us a book called *Love Does*. Bill is asking if I'd like him to read to me. Sure. He and the boys are laughing out loud. Not sure why. I may have to re-read that chapter. I'm glad they have something to do.

*   *   *

Do you have old plates and screws? Wow, it's a wonder he can read my chicken-scratch. My husband is reaching over to the bay window seat that has fast become a storage shelf for papers and clothing. Why is he grabbing a specimen jar? I asked about my original implants.

When I asked Dr. Psutka back at my original consultation if I could keep my current metal plates he paused, looked perplexed and said, "That's an unusual request but I don't see why not. Just ask one of the surgical nurses to set them aside for you."

I responded with, "I promise I won't put them in a shadow box and hang them on the wall."

And now Bill is unscrewing that orange lid. They must be in there. Maybe now someone can tell me what they are made of! Oh, wow. There they are. No screws, just the metal. They are so small, curved and thin. How could something less than an inch in any direction have given me 30 years of relative pain-free life and then too many years of agony? You can put them away now. That's what I want my hands to say. That's enough.

*   *   *

"Mrs. Strom. I'm going to help you have a shower now that your bandages are off. "

A shower sounds heavenly. There goes my Pebbles look with the single tuft of curl on top of my head. I won't miss it. And exactly how am I going to shower? There's nothing in my room. Oh, we're going to walk down the hall to a shower room. I'm not sure I feel stable enough to do this. I really don't want to be left alone in here.

"Would you like me to stay and help you?" the kind nurse asks.

This is no time to be a hero or too shy to accept assistance. "Yshh. Pleesh."

It's too much work to ask. Maybe she plays charades too. I'm pointing to the one-inch strips of white gauze tape stuck tightly over each of my four incisions, two on the neck and two directly in front of my ears, extending up to my temples.

"It's okay if they get wet. We'll just pat them dry when you're finished." She does understand sign language.

And here I thought I wouldn't be able to shower until my stitches were out. Guess I won't need the dry shampoo after all.

I'm exhausted. Who knew a shower could be so taxing?

* * *

I'm so thankful Bill is communicating with people via Caring-Bridge to let them know how I am. Before we left BC, someone introduced us to this website designed to provide easy information sharing for people in medical situations. We have about 100 people who asked to be included in the private updates—such a gift to have this praying community.

I don't want anyone to worry, and having information helps. Bill has let people know that Dr. Psutka says I "look great" and have "less swelling than expected." Good thing. I'm not sure my skin would expand any more. Being the detail guy he is, he also noted the exponential growth in the length of my walks today, from 40 feet to 80 feet to 120 feet to the fourth tour being over 200 feet. Wow, look at me go!

Bill tells me he also shared a post-surgery picture of bleary-eyed me sporting my round-the-face bandages, something I thought we had agreed he would not do. Oh well. This is not the time to worry about looks and perhaps it will help people know how to pray more specifically.

Yes, I did register that I can go home tomorrow. You'll be here to pick me up at 8:00 a.m.? Wow, that's early. All I can do is smile. Sure, I'll be ready. Whatever that means.

* * *

It seems I'm getting my marching orders but we're not moving at a blistering pace. Bill took the prescription list to the hospital pharmacy. He has collected my bottles of distilled water and hydrogen peroxide, the combination I am ordered to rinse with several times a day. The idea of putting peroxide in my mouth is weird. Obviously it's not dangerous but I had no idea it would be the mouthwash and tooth cleanser of choice for post-surgery, teeth-wired-shut, oral hygiene. It must work. It tastes horrible.

My hospital belongings are ready to go. I'm dressed. Bill has not returned from the drug run yet. Every prescription has to be filled in a liquid. Apparently the pharmacist didn't get that memo and initially gave me horse-pill sized antibiotics. I can't imagine sliding those along my cheek and behind my teeth. A few months ago I tried swallowing my tiny Cortef pill while holding my teeth together. I thought I was practicing for this day. Ha! I didn't take into account the incredible amount of swelling inside my mouth. Nothing slides easily anywhere at the moment.

And my teeth feel like they aren't where they used to be. Oh well, nothing feels normal right now, including the absence of pain. I have no pain. I haven't had anything stronger than Advil—and that's for the swelling—since the morphine pump came out. I. Have. No. Pain. In. My. Jaw. Unbelievable.

* * *

Home. Well, temporary, Mississauga, condo, home. On the 32nd floor. Such a beautiful view and tucked away from the world. I feel so grateful for this place to recover.

Bill is busy in the kitchen setting up his system. I like that I can be propped up on this hide-a-bed in the living room. It feels like I can rest and be part of the life we have here. He's working on a medication chart. It reminds me of our early days of marriage when semester end approached and he would count all the assignments he needed to mark, assign a time per paper, calculate the number of hours to complete them all and then create a calendar with blocks of time chunked out to do the work. Those 'organized professor' skills are proving transferable.

I must have dozed off. What's that noise? A whirring. Oh, the blender. The one my sister just happened to have stored away and was eager to give to us. She drove it out to our home months ago so we could start practicing the art of liquid food. Her comment while handing over the high-end machine makes me smile. "Sister, this baby has a motor that could power a small boat!"

Bill is committed to making sure I get enough protein and calories. I've seen him studying the *Guide to Post-jaw Surgery Nutrition*. My healing will not progress as quickly if I lose more than 10% of my body weight, I'm told. I worked hard for the last six months and managed to add five or six extra pounds to give myself a little leeway. I have no scales here to know for sure but I'd guess I've dropped close to ten pounds already. Hospital clear broth didn't exactly stick to my ribs. With a start weight of 125 pounds I don't have much more room to play with.

I can see why people don't want to eat. It's cumbersome and awkward and easier to just skip it. I can't imagine how I would do this without Bill's help. I can already tell he's a top candidate for 'Blender Chef of the Year.' This smoothie à la syringe is delicious. Thank you. Thank you.

*   *   *

No, I don't want to go into the master bedroom tonight. I want to sleep here in the living room propped up. I don't want to share a bed but I don't want to be too far away. He's been sleeping in the guest room, just off the living room. I'm not particularly anxious about being out of the hospital, just want to make sure he can hear me if I need help. At least for this first night.

Sleeping apart isn't new for us. It's been well over a year since we routinely shared a bed. My nights have been so interrupted with pain and difficulty finding comfortable positions that I'm not a great bed-mate. I think the stress of my condition shows up in Bill's dreams causing him to flail and kick unpredictably. It was a bad combination.

We established a new bedtime routine that most nights saw me heading down the hall by 10:00 and Bill climbing in beside me. We'd chat for a few minutes and many evenings he slathered my neck, shoulders and mid-back with anti-inflammatory cream. A kiss goodnight and each found our way to morning across the hall from one another. I'm so grateful that he's willing to make things work, even in the most challenging circumstances. For better or worse, in sickness and in health…

For now, sleep.

* * *

I. Need. Help!

I don't know what's happening. I'm going to drown in my saliva. It's pouring into my mouth. I can't swallow fast enough. William! So hard to talk through teeth. All this water. Can't breathe. *Don't panic. In through nose. Out through nose.* Can't spit. How do I get rid of all this? Gulping. "Pls git me Corteff."

"Are you sure Cortef is the answer? Is it going to help with saliva? Should I call the hospital?"

Of course he would wonder these things. This is what we do in our marriage. We discuss a situation to gain understanding. We ask questions and try to hear each other's perspectives. Not now! This is not the time for talk. I need medication now! I'm starting to panic. *Stop. Calm yourself. Breathe.*

"Won't madder iff I'n ded!" Sorry. He looks hurt. Have to sort that out later. Need medication. That got his attention. He's filling the syringe. *Breathe. Swallow. Breathe. Swallow. Keep breathing. Oh God, I've come so far. Please, don't let me drown now.*

Swallow the drugs. Swallow. Swallow. Just keep swallowing.

Yes, it's getting better. I can manage it now. Still a lot. Don't understand why. *Swallow, relax.* Not gulping and gasping anymore. Thank you. Thank you, God. Yes, I'll try to sleep now. I wonder how this post will read on CaringBridge.

* * *

This is not a "stay in bed and recover surgery." I have been told to get up and move around multiple times throughout the day. I understand the thinking when I recall how weak my being felt simply getting out of bed that first time. But soon I could get to the bathroom without fear of passing out and my jaunts in the hospital grew.

Now that we're in our condo-away-from-home we have new landmarks of progress; like the first morning I made it out our door, down the elevator (holding tightly to the handrail for the 32-floor ride), into the lobby and out the front exit to the first flowerbed. In total I maybe walked 50 feet. Felt like a marathon.

Later that day we repeated the route and went a few feet beyond. Soon we celebrated arrival at the second flowerbed and already I see a routine developing. It seems that two walks a day will become our norm, including shared elevator rides with people giving sideways glances at my odd face.

* * *

Bill has been so faithful in writing posts on CaringBridge to keep our far-away people up to date on my progress. He documented each day since our arrival and family and friends have flooded us with comments, scripture and encouragement, which he has read to me. And today, I surprised our faithful readers by authoring this post.

On June 2, 2014, I wrote:

A Reprieve

Good morning, faithful team! I have the privilege of writing the update this morning while my amazing caregiver makes breakfast. I think his next book will be called *101 Delicious Ways to Eat from a Tube!* Not only is he providing me with variety but he's making sure I get enough calories and nutrients. He's even a little bossy at times about needing to eat more. :) Can't imagine doing this journey without him.

I do believe that these days are an oasis of sorts as my swelling decreases, my sleep improves and I have not yet had to begin the hourly routine of stretching my jaw open. I have been off morphine since before leaving the hospital—not because I'm being a hero—but rather because the intensity of pre-surgery pain is simply gone. My best explanation is in the doctor saying my joints were "extremely arthritic." Take out troubled joints and you take the pain with it, I guess. Considering all that's been done, it is still shocking to me that the pain I was living with before rates so much higher than what I have now, only five days post-operatively.

I recall someone saying they were praying that at every turn there would be "better thans, unexpecteds, not typicals," and I've heard a lot of that. Apparently I've had less swelling than normal, although honestly, I'm not sure where more would have gone! I asked Taylor and Clark which cartoon character they thought I resembled and while they couldn't come up with a cartoon, they agreed that Jay Leno came to mind. Be careful what you ask for! ☺ I was also expecting much more bruising, and while the IV sites on my arm are black and horrific-looking, my face is only hint-o-green today. It's not a huge concern to me as my social circle is pretty small.

Well, it's almost time for my post-breakfast nap. Thank you again and again for your prayers and words of encouragement. It makes being far away seem less so. The ways in which God has gone before and is meeting us in the midst are too many to account for here. Just know that He is faithful and we are thankful!

With a full heart,

Shelaine

* * *

My Abbotsford friend, Sue, arrived yesterday with a heart to be near and endure my wired-shut state. I wrote notes and tried out ventriloquism skills while she talked and together we watched *The No. 1 Ladies' Detective Agency.* Bill spent his 'free time' scouring the city for replacement ice packs so I can continue sporting my round-the-head bonnet of cooling.

The friend-time nourished my soul and provided me with a new insight—trying to converse exhausts my face! I had no idea how much effort it would take to communicate without jaw movement.

* * *

Bill and I both woke up this morning with a similar Caring-Bridge post idea so we combined his list of "10 Things We Didn't Know A Month Ago" and my "A Collection of Random Things You May or May Not Find Interesting" to create "A Joint Entry":

1. Total jaw joint replacement surgery requires perpetual follow up. Practically speaking, that means at least one trip to ON per year.

2. Hospitals are all the same from granite floors to heavy doors and pokey elevators. Credit Valley's unique feature—all departments use the Second Cup as a key reference point for giving directions.

3. You can get lost in a hospital. Even on day 4.

4. Prior to surgery, I was required to stop taking Omega 3 and stop using Voltaren anti-inflammatory cream as both are known to have mild blood thinning properties. The day after surgery they loaded me with blood thinners. Timing.

5. City living has different parking requirements. The higher you live, the lower you park. It takes a full 8 minutes of swirling up and out to leave our parkade. (Yes, he timed it!)

6. You can't lick your lips with a wired jaw. Nor are you supposed to sneeze, suck, blow your nose or brush your teeth. You must, however, maintain meticulous oral hygiene by rinsing every 2 hours with a saline/peroxide mix.

7. Clark thought a different rendition of this city's name worked better. We now reside in "Miss-a-sausage."

8. There's just no point trying to explain to strangers crossing the street why I look like I do.

9. Eric arrives tonight for a weekend visit and will join us at my appointment with Dr. Psutka tomorrow afternoon. He and Bill will take in a Blue Jays baseball game on Sunday afternoon.

10. Please pray for my first appointment with the surgeon tomorrow. Our sense is that all is progressing far better than we could have ever hoped for or imagined. Love to you all!

* * *

A friend sent us a message commenting on the upbeat nature of our CaringBridge posts and also included her sense that there are likely hard places too. It caught me a little off guard and I wondered if others believe we're only telling the good parts of our story. Yes and no.

In the big picture, I would concede that moving to Mississauga for an unknown period of time to undergo a major surgery, leaving family and friends, is hard. Having teeth wired shut and not being able to talk (or be understood) with ease is hard. Sleeping propped up so I'm never on my side is hard. Eating blenderized everything is hard.

It's just not *all that hard*. And this is where I would say God has used the last two years to prepare us for this season. Hard is relative and closely connected to what we make our focus. Living in the heart of a city is something we have never done together so it feels like an adventure. I am on the other side of the surgery that went extremely well—a procedure that has taken my daily pain score from seven or eight to one or two. That isn't hard, that's hope!

We have so much to be thankful for. The timing of this operation coinciding with Bill being done teaching; Trinity Western blessing him to do his research and writing from afar; our kids coming to visit; finances being a non-stress; no complications from surgery; literally thousands of people praying for us... We're enjoying good humor, great food, lovely company, beautiful weather, and we're not waiting anymore. We're actually doing this. That's huge!

Bill weighed in on the topic as well, sharing these thoughts on CaringBridge:

> For me the new normal has meant spending more time with Shelaine than I usually would this time of year. In late May and early June I normally ramp up my research and writing as I commute regularly to TWU. This year I am chipping away at reading and writing about three hours a day on the works of Menno Simons and how his theology and practices might enlighten us about communication. My "office" is the common party room downstairs and the dining room table.
>
> I might also do some fishing back home this time of year, but not here. But not without temptation! The Credit River flows 15 minutes from our complex. If you YouTube "catching salmon on the Credit River" you may marvel at the large fish that migrate up and down this waterway to Lake Ontario. (For keeners, they are Steelhead, and more catchable than the ones in the Chilliwack River.) But having no gear, I've resigned myself to fish later in BC when the sockeye run is promising to be strong.
>
> No doubt my roles in the kitchen as head cook and bottle washer are not like BC. But I do cook back home, and

Shelaine and I often cook together. So to become the primary cook, for her benefit, for this season, has been fine. It may take longer than usual to prepare our meals, and giving out medicine almost every two hours takes some mindfulness. But hey, this is all for my best friend, who needs me, and I know she would do the same for me if I were in the same place.

In the end this 'difficult time' is what we make of it. I am thankful that my work gives me four weeks holidays in summer and that I can pick and choose when to take them. As a couple, there are new dynamics of care and concern we can knit together here unlike at home. While I would not wish harm or illness on anyone, such hardships can bring closeness between people if you roll with them and lean on God's resources to make it through. Some of you reading this know the same.

* * *

I have become quite accustomed to children staring at my face as we ride the elevator, or adults stealing a peek, hoping I didn't notice. I was not, however, prepared for similar behavior from the staff at Dr. Psutka's office yesterday.

I approached the desk upon arrival and waited for one of the four receptionists to be free. After a few seconds, one looked up and said, "You are?" to which I replied, "Shhlane Shhtrmm" (killer name for a wired jaw!). She glanced down at her register and looked up at me quizzically. "Sorry, what's your name?" I repeated my best effort at "Shh's" and she said, "Okay.....well, okay. I...I'll be doing your x-rays soon. Have a seat for a moment."

My waiting room vantage point gave me full view of staff going about their work and periodically stopping, glancing my way, whispering and carrying on. I was beginning to wonder if it was my new hairdo.

"Shelaine, I'm ready to do your x-rays now. Please come this way."

I followed the same technician who signed me in down the hall to the little x-ray room. She reached for the lead apron and as she placed it on my shoulders said, "I have never seen a patient so upbeat and doing so well only a week after surgery!" I couldn't help but smile for the camera.

Leaving that room I encountered Dr. Psutka in the hall. "Wow, look at you! You look great!" It kind of makes me wonder if dress code for one week post-surgery is pajamas. I didn't get that memo.

Next step was suture removal where Bill and Eric joined me, the surgeon, and a nurse in a small dental room. The nurse removed my steri-strip bandages and the tightening band of what I thought had been tensing muscles vanished immediately. She apologized profusely for the pain she caused but all I felt was tape stuck to hair.

Dr. Psutka explained my x-rays and showed us all my 'new look.' The prostheses are positioned exactly where they need to be and my bite is aligned perfectly.

As he "unwired" me (which really meant 10 seconds of removing heavy duty rubber bands from hooks on the surgical braces), he asked, "How's your pain compared to before surgery?"

I motioned with my hand to show "way lower."

"Pain killers?" he asked.

"None." I mumbled, to which he replied, "Those who have immediate pain reduction have the best chance of doing well long term." Then he smiled, slid his chair back and said, "Well, you are certainly the poster person around here!"

I now sport only two light-weight, stretchy rubber bands, reminiscent of the kind all three sons wore during their days with braces. They prevent dislocation while allowing further healing and a limited range of motion (not a bad idea since I could be prone to throwing my mouth wide open to rejoice and give thanks to God!). I take them off to eat—yes, regular soft food off a fork! My mandate is then to do 25 stretches to a one-knuckle opening, something I could do with ease by this morning.

Oh, and I can talk better now, too.

At supper last night I kept being aware of Bill, sitting beside me watching me eat. Each time I turned he wore a huge grin. That's okay, go ahead and stare.

It seems our CaringBridge following share our excitement as comments of praise and delight like these are populating the site.

This is the "exceeding, abundant, above all we can ask or think." We are rejoicing and relieved WITH you!! (Ruth)

Praise God from whom all blessings flow! We are rejoicing with you, shouting songs of praise for this miracle! (Bev)

I look forward to hearing from both of you every day! Your progress and healing is amazing, and can hardly wait to hear all about it in person! And you are even able to do the jaw-stretching exercises - PTL! (Marilyn H.)

Wow! Thank you, Lord for showing your love and power far beyond our wildest expectations! And thank you, Bill & Shelaine for taking us along for the ride. Tears of joy are flowing freely here in Abbotsford. (Marilyn I.)

* * *

Bill and I are developing a rhythm to our days and finding this isolated time together meaningful beyond anything we anticipated. We have long enjoyed each other's company but the uncertainty of an invasive procedure and recovery loomed before us. Perhaps part of our jovial spirit is rooted in surgery being over. Whatever the cause, we had fun putting together this CaringBridge post on June 8, 2014:

You Know You're in Southern Ontario When...

This is Bill, and I couldn't help but have some fun in today's post. For all of those who grew up in Southern Ontario, my apologies. These ideas were just asking to be expressed. (At the end of today's post we do note two important prayer requests.)

1. You are allowed to drive on any highway you wish, as long as its number begins with a 4.
2. The sports stores in the mall offer 40 styles of Blue Jay caps, 25 for the Toronto Maple Leafs, and two for Canucks.
3. You buy and pour your milk from a plastic bag.
4. The roads don't run east and west. They run perpendicular to Lake Ontario, which runs Southwest by Northeast. (Which is why I drive with my head off to the side.)

5. You get lost, so you look for a landmark mountain. You stay lost.

6. You get lost so you look for the 40-storey highrises in downtown Mississauga, and you know right where you are.

7. Daffodils bloom in late May.

8. The favourite phrase after church is, "Chalet?"

9. You would love to take a drive in the open countryside, but can't afford the tank of gas to find some and get back home.

10. The posted start time for a Kings vs. Rangers game lines up with your watch.

Okay, so I'll never make it to late night comedy, but perhaps Sunday morning smiles.

On a more serious note, we ask that you pray regarding the wear and tear of the metal braces on Shelaine's mouth. Now that she can talk, her lips rub more and more on the steel framework that runs along the gum lines of both top and bottom teeth. The back sides of her lips are becoming torn up and we want to guard against infection. We need to get wax to cover the sharp metal.

The other issue regards managing the new dynamic of energy. Pre-surgery she would start the day pretty strong and then gradually worsen during the day. Now she goes from energy to none in very short order. So please pray for a wise plan to increase activity which allows strength and stamina to grow.

All our love,

Bill

*   *   *

It's an odd sensation to feel like the bottom third of my face is a stranger. I've decided that I need to approach this jaw like a new friend. It's going to take time to get know each other and I'm sure there will be many things I love about it... and perhaps a few annoyances as well.

On Friday when the heavy duty bands came off and the doctor asked me to open up, my brain knew what that meant but the sensation of disconnect was real. My lips and teeth parted but I had no concept of whether I had opened 1 mm or 10. Weird.

Funnier was my first meal. Again, the disconnect around how wide I was opening my mouth has meant lots of fork-hits-teeth, food falls off, too much food on fork, food everywhere. You get the picture. Periodically I did get food in and then experienced a, "who's chewing that?" phenomenon.

Part of what I now realize I'm doing is getting to know one of the limitations of my new friend. When Dr. Psutka cut the bone segment out he had to detach the lateral pterygoid muscle as well. There is no means of re-attaching muscles to metal so anything that requires a side-to-side grinding or front-to-back gliding motion is lost. I knew this going in, of course, but it's difficult to isolate what that movement affects when it's working. I'm getting a better picture now. When we take a sip of tea, apparently we slide our bottom jaw slightly forward as the top lip wraps over the cup's edge. If you don't, drool happens! Remarkably and thankfully, our brains are highly adaptable and I can already see adjustments that are proving hopeful for not having to eat and drink with a bib from this day forward.

Chewing is another new world. It's hard to tell what relates to a mouth full of metal and when to credit my missing pterygoid. Whatever the case, I know I put food into my mouth but for the life of me I can't figure out where it goes. Brain, tongue, teeth and jaw need to have a team meeting! The net effect is long, leisurely meal times.

My new friend is a bit noisy, too. When I walk, my teeth clatter around, reminiscent of my great grandmother and her false teeth. Bill assures me that I'm the only one who hears it. I also hear new noises and maybe it's just because I know there's a lot of metal in there, but it sounds distinctly like Cobalt Chromium Alloy to me.

The inside of my lips are a war zone of swelling, gouge marks and broken skin. Wax on the braces saved the day and I've found some relief from the discomfort of sharp metal and allowing skin to heal. I'm grateful.

Overall, I still marvel at how little pain I experience. Everything is relative to pre-op pain and nothing even comes close to matching that mark. Yesterday, as my new physiotherapist and I discussed a similar topic, he smiled and said, "But remember, that's because of your pain killers." When I clarified that I'm not on any pain killers, he joined the ranks of those amazed by my recovery. I have to say, after so many years of being a medical/dental anomaly for all the wrong reasons, being on this side of "abnormal" is a lot of fun!

This new physiotherapist was described to me months ago as the "Egyptian Magician who Loves the Lord" and is yet another reminder of God's intimate care and provision. Raafat Rofail's practice is two blocks off Lake Ontario, only 12 minutes from our place. We continue to see evidence of God going before us in every category, which is important to dwell on as I face the realities of rehabilitation.

Physiotherapy felt akin to poking a sleeping bear. There is much hard work ahead to realign and strengthen all my muscles as they have adapted over the years to improper positioning, quite literally from head to toe. I am eager and ready to do this kind of work though—just not too much and not quite yet. This week I'm feeling more fully the fatigue of major surgery and am being careful to keep life quiet. The good news is...I really don't have anything else to do!

*   *   *

Actually, I did have something to do. Last night—exactly two weeks post-surgery—Bill and I attended a gala event which, given my chubby face, brace-lined teeth and funky hairdo, seemed a stretch.

You may recall that one year into my season of writing and anticipating surgery, I submitted an article to Truth Media. My first publication, "Waiting: A Passionate Pause" came online in May 2013.

About four weeks ago I was notified that The Word Guild (a national Christian writers association) had shortlisted this article for an award and that I was invited to the black-tie Awards Gala which was to be held—get this—in Mississauga on June 11th, a short ten minute drive from our condo. I felt honored to be shortlisted but knew it would only be 14 days after surgery. I figured I'd be 'black eye', not 'black tie' ready. Bill and I decided that he would go and we'd find a sitter for me.

As we now know, God has a different trajectory for this recovery than any of us expected. Last night Bill and I were able to attend the event together! I hadn't packed a lot of evening gowns for this trip nor did Bill bring a suit. However, thanks to my personal shoppers, Bill and Eric, and our friend Joanne with her mobile-suit-and-accessory delivery service, I think we looked pretty good! It felt like an enormous gift and victory in itself simply to be at the event. It was a wonderful, God-honoring evening.

And, wonder of wonders, I won. We were over the moon with excitement and gratitude as I was awarded the honor of Best Article in the Personal Experience category for 2013. It felt so appropriate that Bill and I share that moment together as he has been my biggest fan and faithful editor. One beautiful gift of this season of pain has been our now shared love of writing, reading each other's work and spending many Saturday mornings by our fire having what we've come to call 'mutual edit-fication' sessions.

I even gave a short acceptance speech.

*　*　*

I have done enough research on this procedure to know this day was coming, I just didn't know when nor could I have anticipated the intensity of pain.

Yesterday afternoon, June 13th, we met with Dr. Psutka and he entered the room with, "You're smiling!" Indeed I was —so broadly, in fact, that I had to unhook my top lip off my braces. Classy, but I suspect he's seen that look before. He measured my mouth opening—15 mm—and felt the joints opening and closing. "Perfect," he declared.

Upon checking my bite, he decided to rearrange my rubber bands in order to pull my left-side teeth down so they fully meet the bottom teeth like the right side does. For any of you who have had braces or have had kids with braces you'll know this is pretty standard practice and no big deal. (As long as I can remember where the bands go!)

Then Dr. Psutka announced that I am ready to start opening my mouth. Enter my new "friend." It's called a Therabite and another patient in the waiting room dubbed it a "modern torture device." Dr. Psutka set it for 20mm (meaning he expects my mouth opening to increase by 5 mm over this next week) and instructed me to use it four times a day, 25 repetitions each time.

Our appointment ended with him extending his hand and saying, "You're doing great. I'm really proud of you."

And now I have experienced the Therabite first hand. After dinner I put the device between my teeth and began to squeeze the handle, which pushes one plate up, one down, forcing my mouth open, tearing scar tissue. I. Felt. Pain. Agonizing fire ripped through my joints. Bill stood beside me providing a watchful eye as I willed myself to squeeze and inflict more excruciating pain. Twenty-five times.

Honestly, *this* is what I've been expecting all along. I am incredibly grateful for the two weeks I've had to grow stronger from the surgery before embarking on this portion of recovery. The piece I hadn't anticipated is the counter-intuitive mental battle that rages when I must *intentionally* generate that much pain! I am keenly aware of my need to trust the surgeon and follow his instructions. And, I know that I get to choose. On so many levels, it doesn't make sense to do what I'm doing.

But it does make sense in the big picture because a joint that does not have full range of motion will be a joint with pain. I awoke early this morning and found myself reflecting on the phrase "modern torture device" and decided that's not the approach I want to take for this next step. God has faithfully provided all along and I choose to trust Him for the strength and courage to do this gruelling work. Also, when I asked Dr. Psutka how long I would use the Therabite, he replied, "For the rest of your life. It will become part of your daily routine."

This new companion of mine, while causing so much pain now, is part of my team working toward strengthening, healing and full recovery. Why would I want an adversarial relationship with something on my side? Clearly the only sensible approach is to welcome it on board by giving it a name.

We are posting a picture of the device and asking our CaringBridge crowd for input. There may even be a prize.

* * *

Gertrude, Helga, Termineator, Jaws of Clay, Jaws of Life, Theophilus, Bruce—after the nickname given to the mechanical shark in Jaws; Trudy or Gertrude which means spear of strength; Jaws, Jawbreaker, BFF, Gumbo, Dynamos; Ethel Junina, The Pain Machine. There is no shortage of creativity among our friends!

And the winner is: Maxilla, primarily because of the rationale given by Barb, an English teacher. "Maxilla or Max, for short, can be a triple-entendre. It's denotative meaning is 'jaw'; you want to open to the 'max'; it sounds eerily like 'godzilla.'" And so it is. The Therabite shall forever more be referred to as Maxilla.

The little contest has been a great source of levity during this new requirement of self-induced pain. I recall the doctor who berated me for my struggle to describe my pain and now look back with appreciation for one redeeming feature of the experience—he gave me a descriptive language. And because of that day, I have been able to be much more specific in how I relate what's going on in my body to each medical person I encounter.

The pain I am experiencing now is categorically different than what I had before surgery.

The day of my pre-operation tests was the last time I described my usual pain. For the last four years it has been aching, gnawing, burning, sharp, shooting, sickening, splitting, stabbing, throbbing, exhausting, continuous pain ranking on average an 8 on a scale of 1–10 (10 being worst pain ever). It was relentless and although my body was doing exactly what it should have—notifying me that there was a major problem —the pain felt pointless.

Immediately after surgery, nothing (and I really mean nothing) has come even close to that earlier level. I don't think I've used a rating higher than a three or four and that was in the hospital when my back was screaming from immobility. Nothing related to my jaw has ranked over a two.

And then came time to poke that sleeping bear...

There's really no pleasant way to describe stretching my jaw. When I squeeze Maxilla open the searing pain is immediate, nauseating and it ranks 9–10 every time. It takes my breath away and leaves me weak and in a cold sweat. As soon as I release the Therabite, the searing pain goes away to leave only a dull, aching echo. Cumulatively, however, it's exhausting.

But here's the difference. This is constructive pain that will, by God's grace, give me years of living without the continuous daily pain I had before surgery. It does subside an hour or so after each session so I still have windows in my day where I'm back at the 0–2 end of the pain scale. And it's proactive pain, not pain maintained—a huge motivator for me to pick up that device and squeeze.

I am grateful for all that my years of pre-surgery pain management taught me. I feel well prepared and ready for this challenge. As awful as it is, I'm doing something active and am already, after two short days, seeing progress. I am able to open about 4–5 mm wider, and eating supper last night felt far more "normal." I think even that small increase in mobility in the joint made it easier to chew and swallow, although it's hard to say for sure because my swelling is so much less now as well.

And just when I thought I was being sufficiently stretched… the fire alarm went off and we had to evacuate the building from our lovely vantage point on the 32nd floor. Bill and I are giving thanks that our required walk down 64 flights of stairs (seven steps per flight) didn't happen two weeks ago! There was no fire but the HVAC unit malfunctioned and set off the alarm. All is well. Except my calves. They are stiff already.

* * *

Friends have been a life-line to Bill and me in general and specifically in this jaw season. Wendy is no exception and she arrived from Abbotsford with her purse full of nail polish, each bottle from a different girlfriend in British Columbia who wanted to show her love in a tangible, colorful way. By the end of the pedicure my toes were hard to miss—left to right—sparkly gold, lavender, salmon, mint, fire-engine red, royal purple, orange, teal, pink and burgundy. I'm glad it's sandal weather.

My vibrant feet created a welcomed distraction from my funny face and were the first thing Katie, the kiniseologist at Rafaat's office, noticed when I went for yet another double-slot appointment that 'happened' to open up in the schedule of a practitioner for whom people wait months to see.

As the physio session ended, Rafaat asked me again when I was planning to leave Ontario. I responded with, "likely the end of June," to which he replied, "I hope you can stay longer. I can help you with your jaw but it needs more time to heal first." My heart sank a little as I would love to continue working with this gentle man who has seen me from early in the post-surgery days and is highly skilled at his craft. I expressed my mild disappointment to Bill as we drove back to the condo and we concluded that, once again, we need to trust God for each step.

Upon return home, I checked my email to find a note from Joanne, my surgeon's office administrator, saying that Dr. Psutka would like me to stay until mid-July so he can be the one to remove my arch bars (apparently that's what my funky braces are really called). Mid-July. Interesting. Both Bill and I felt surprised by the news. His comment was something like, "Another month? That feels like a long time!" My sentiment was similar but I admit, I felt relief as well, most obviously because I can continue to work with this physiotherapist a while longer. But that wasn't the only reason.

Taking these arch bars off is not the same as having regular braces removed. I will require another general anesthetic and since this team is now so familiar with my entire medical history, it feels comforting to know they will be the ones facilitating this step. This procedure is booked for July 10th.

And if I'm really honest, perhaps staying here until mid-July is another protection from the Lord...from myself! I know that when I return to Abbotsford I will want to have tea with everyone. I suspect that's not a great idea since I find talking exhausting. It really is ideal to be communicating in writing during this season, one more way God went before and sent me to another province for surgery.

We knew coming into this that staying 4–6 weeks post-surgery was the requirement and June 30th is only four and a half weeks. Our condo rental ends June 30th so we naively hoped not to have to extend the agreement. Alas, we do.

We sorted through the implications of being here until mid-July and found out our two-bedroom condo is no longer available after the 30th. However, we can move into a one-bedroom within the complex. Once we had some time to groan a little at the inconvenience of moving, we reflected on the timing of our sons' visits and the reality that we no longer have need for the larger unit. We also realized that we don't have to pack but rather get the building's luggage cart and simply wheel our belongings to the new floor. Another adventure with a different view.

* * *

One of the many unexpected blessings of our experience is the weekly house cleaning service included in our condo rental.

I am grateful that Bill does not have that role in addition to being nurse, cook, book reader, driver, grocery shopper and general entertainment provider to the surgically recovering.

We've come to learn that the policy of the condo management team is that no housekeeper will ever be left alone, which protects all parties involved from accusations of theft. As a result, each Wednesday morning Monika (the Rental Coordinator) and Colleen (Wonder Woman of all things clean) arrive with their wire carts-on-wheels full of supplies and fresh linens. Colleen dives into her work and Monika engages in conversation to make sure our needs are met.

When Sue visited us at one week post-surgery, I did my best to introduce everyone through my wired teeth. The women picked up the conversation and Monika soon learned that Sue is a friend from BC who flew out to visit me and help Bill with my care. Monika's astonished reply, "What? It's one thing to have friends who are willing to come party with you, but to have friends come when you are in need? That's unheard of in this day and age. It gives me goose bumps."

Yesterday the twosome arrived in a similar manner, commenting on how much my swelling has decreased in the past week. Monika and I chatted about several topics and then she proclaimed, "You are so relaxed. I can't believe it. I work with Dr. Psutka's patients all the time and all the others have been so stressed and tense. I can't believe you are so calm!"

I smiled and replied, "Well Monika, we do have hundreds of people praying for us." From there we had a meaningful conversation about the faith community journeying with us.

As I reflected on the interaction, the account of friends bringing a paralyzed man to Jesus came to mind. Those friends carried him on a mat and went to great lengths to dig through a roof and lower him into the center of the crowd, right in front of Jesus. (Mark 2:4) These faithful people knew exactly where their friend needed to be taken.

I find myself identifying with the guy on the mat. I wonder if he asked his friends to carry him or if they simply came over one day and said, "Hold on, we're taking you on a trip!"

If the latter was the case, I can imagine him having a few questions, perhaps because I have had many along my journey. Over a year ago, I agonized over whether or not to put a prayer request in our church bulletin. I knew I needed prayer and I wanted people to pray. But even my teaching background couldn't negate my dislike for the attention such announcements bring.

I argued with myself claiming I had a great network of close friends praying. Wasn't that enough? Then a few wise friends, independent of one another, and all within a short span, strongly encouraged me to enlarge our prayer base. I am so grateful we did and could never have imagined how widely the circle would expand. We know of several churches and prayer networks around the world lowering us to the feet of Jesus.

* * *

On June 20, 2014 I wrote this CaringBridge post:

Good morning, all,

A couple of months after I received news that I would require this surgery I checked in with my trusted counsellor.

I reviewed the serious risks of the procedure, decisions to be made and named some of my fears attached to it all. Later in the session he encouraged me to simply live out the experience, one moment at a time and not stress over "doing surgery well." I recall smiling and replying, "You mean I don't have to blog my way through the process?"

Little did I know at that point how central writing would be to my recovery.

I had many available hours in the two+ years between work ending and my surgery date. In that period, I developed a routine that likely kept me sane. At 7:00 a.m. I sipped tea and by 7:30 began writing. I worked at a table set up near the fireplace with a view of our backyard. I often wrote until ten or later and more often marveled at the joy I found in this creative, solitary venture that let my jaw rest.

Not surprisingly, I suppose, I find myself gravitating back to a similar life-giving routine. Our mornings here are developing a rhythm where, by 7:30-ish breakfast is finished, Maxilla and I have bonded and Bill and I head to our separate spaces. I sit at a desk we've moved in front of our bank of windows overlooking the city, a green space and Lake Ontario on the horizon.

But there is a much bigger value for me in CaringBridge than simply writing. It often felt like a curiosity that we should be blessed with an incredibly supportive community and then be required to leave everyone behind and live four provinces away for two months. Thankfully, we had traveled far enough on this road to trust God.

Being able to write provides a sense of meaningful connection, something I highly value. Comments have been a lifeline of encouragement, often focusing on key needs for that day. And let's be honest, it's much more delightful to be a writer if you have readers!

Practically speaking, I simply can't talk much yet. Yesterday was a physio day, and while the treatment invigorated me, the discussion with receptionist, kinesiologist and physiotherapist likely doubled my daily word output and left me worn out. It also chewed up the inside of my lips again from the extra flesh-rubbing-on-metal demand. Back to wax today!

And on a prayer note, we're off to see Dr. Psutka this afternoon. I have every reason to believe he will be pleased with my progress given that I can reach his prescribed maximum opening on 22 of 25 stretches now and hold each one for several seconds. And, you know where this is going. Having met this goal likely means a new one will be set today of stretching into wider agonizing space. Thankfully, I'm not dreading the idea because I now know I can endure it and I know that hard work in these days will reap years of benefit. That said, please do pray. It really hurts!

We trust you will have a great day. Blessings on each of you for loving us so well.

With love and gratitude,

Shelaine

*   *   *

Yesterday morning we walked through our neighborhood and found a new trail which is much less urban and full of cattails, a stream and green space—a refreshing change from busy city streets. We were out for 90 minutes, which I must qualify slightly as there did happen to be a Starbucks on our return route. None the less, I am able to walk 40+ minutes at a time now. Too bad I can't talk that much.

Our afternoon appointment with Dr. Psutka filled us with information and encouragement. After the standard, "how are you and how's it going with the Therabite" (he's not on a first name basis with "Maxilla" yet), he asked me to demonstrate. I stretched open to the stopping point and held my jaw there for several seconds, 3 or 4 times. He beamed. "That's fantastic!" He grabbed his ruler and announced, "27 millimeters! You rock!"

Dr. Psutka went on to explain that patients who have had multiple jaw surgeries—a club I now hold membership in—do well to reach a 25 mm opening. "But you can open more than that," he stated matter of factly as he adjusted Maxilla. "I know because I did so while you were on the table." With that he demonstrated a two-handed wrenching-open motion.

"How wide was that?" I asked.

"35 mm. So that's what I'm setting the Therabite to." He smiled and handed her back to me as he explained that I would not require any further appointments until July 10th when I return to have the arch bars (braces) off.

"What is it about removing these that requires general anesthetic?" I inquired.

He replied, "It hurts! There's a wire tightly wrapped around every tooth, right at the base, and snipping each one pinches and sometimes cuts the gum. We can do it with freezing but it takes a lot of needles. But five minutes under general anesthetic and you're done." I no longer wonder why my teeth and gums ache.

Before the appointment ended, Bill asked what the long term progression of using Maxilla would be, wondering if I might lessen the number of stretching sessions per day at some point.

Dr. Psutka shook his head. "No, four times a day for the rest of your life."

I have come to understand that one type of pain I experienced pre-surgery—relentless burning—came from lack of range of motion in the joint. Just before I started using Maxilla, I was beginning to feel a distinct tightening and some low grade burn returning. Once stretched, it disappeared.

Granted, stretching has added a whole new world of pain. Those initial stretches into new territory were more intense than labor or kidney stones, but mercifully far shorter in duration. As last week progressed and I routinely opened to my goal of 25 mm, the intensity lessened and my recovery time shortened. Moving toward the 35 mm goal for the first time certainly upped the intensity again but nothing like those first days.

Bill expressed his sadness this morning over my "'til death do us part" relationship with Maxilla news. I know there will be days where Maxilla will have Godzilla qualities. However, just like so many things, it all feels relative to me. I have spent the last three years of my life living with intense levels of pain 24/7. So the idea of 20-25 minutes of daily pain and inconvenience seems a small price to pay for relief. And besides, Maxilla came with her own fashionable zippered blue travel case. I foresee many grand adventures together.

*   *   *

On June 22, 2014, I wrote:

Beavertail:

Definition #1: Addictive whole wheat, hand-stretched pastry that is float cooked in oil then served piping hot covered in cinnamon sugar.

Definition #2: First crunchy, soft-chewy food I've bitten into and chewed since June 2011.

I used to be teased in my workplace for my love of variety and it's true. The thought of soup and smoothies for the rest of my days became one significant motivator for pursuing answers to my jaw crisis. I adopted an "I eat to live, not live to eat" philosophy to cope and worked daily on choosing gratitude for proper nutrition.

Yesterday Bill challenged me to write a post including a list of everything I couldn't eat pre-surgery. The list would be too long, but I did consider the food I craved and couldn't eat yet: All things salad, raw vegetables, fresh fruit, nuts, anything crunchy but particularly chips, and, as much as I don't even love burgers, I longed to open my mouth wide and sink my teeth into bun, chicken, cheese, lettuce, tomatoes, avocado, and dripping BBQ sauce!

And here I am today, three and a half weeks post-surgery with the blessing of Dr. Psutka to eat whatever I'd like! He said that there is enough scar tissue in the muscles now to prevent dislocation from anything except opening too widely. (Trust me, there's no concern of that happening!) So, on Friday night as we wandered around our neighborhood, we bumped into a food truck selling Beavertails, a much raved-about Ontario tradition neither of us had experienced. We sat on Celebration Square stairs and, for the first time in three years and with confidence that I had permission to do so, I sank my teeth into the crunchy, chewy treat, munched it slowly and swallowed.

As a side bar, I can't help observe what these changes mean. Clearly patterns have been established in my brain that say, "When you bite down, pain happens" because I bite and my whole body tenses. But there is no pain! So, brain, it's time to develop some new pathways.

Eating is still awkward, partly because biting into some things pushes the arch bar braces into my already-tender gums. They also prevent my lips from closing completely, increasing drool probability. But those are temporary and once gone I'll have a clearer understanding of how a lack of lateral movement—and grinding motion—affect eating. Even with these restrictions, I have eaten fresh blueberries, strawberries and mangoes. I've bitten into toast, carrots not cooked to mush, stir-fry, and chips. Oh, the bliss of variety and texture. Watch out salads, here I come.

*   *   *

Periodically Bill feels inspired to post on CaringBridge and wrote this piece he called *Stand by Your Woman* for our community.

June 23, 2014

Good morning friends and family,

Bill here to reflect on my experience supporting Shelaine since she began using Maxilla.

Tammy Wynette had it right. Her 1968 hit keeps rolling through my head these days, her twang-y commitment to stand by her man no matter what. It seems right, even if Country Western to me can be so wrong.

When Shelaine's jaw was wired shut, my main tasks were to manage the medicine regimen, deliver ice packs, and man the blender. I cooked, kept kitchen, washed clothes and read books aloud. For a week it was busy, busy, busy.

When the wires came off, and she could speak much more easily, life got back more to normal. Her need for Advil lessened with the swelling decreasing and the antibiotics ran their course. I still made our meals and kept kitchen, but for the second week there was less 'by her side' activity.

Enter Maxilla.

It was one thing to support Shelaine propped up in bed, yet another when she had to begin inflicting self-pain. As you know, after each meal, she goes to that sad place that will bring happiness long term. She eyes herself in the mirror, takes a deep breath, and squeezes the blue calipers. Once, twice, three times, four, and five. She takes a break for ten seconds, then starts up again: one, two, three, four, five. When she first began, she let out agonizing groans after the fifth prying, every time.

And I stand by her.

Initially I did so in case she fainted. We didn't know how she would respond to this new kind of pain. Despite the cries of anguish (even still), we are thankful she has remained clear-headed and stable, though not without breaking a sweat.

I also count the millimeters on the scale on Maxilla's side bar. "That was 25, two 26s, and two 27s." Shelaine can't see the scale when using the device so I call play by play so she knows where she's at.

Of course standing beside her means more than technical support. My new role reminds me of the word paraclete that New Testament writers used to refer to the Holy Spirit in the life of those being regenerated. It comes from two words: "para" (alongside) and "klētos" (from kalein 'to call'). It means God called the Holy Spirit alongside us after Jesus resurrected, to be our comforter and advocate for those who call on him.

Of course there will come a time when I won't be comforting alongside every time, but right now it seems the right thing to do. And I know Shelaine appreciates the short back rubs between reps.

Tammy was right.

Bill

Our family and friends were deeply moved by Bill's perspective and wrote:

> This brings tears to my eyes, Bill and Shelaine. Your unwavering support of each other and genuine caring and comforting is love in action. Bill, you gave us a new perspective of Shelaine's pain—thank you. Shelaine, I pray for courage and endurance for you—it must be so hard to stand there and know what you are about to "do" to yourself. I love you, my friend. (Marilyn)

You two are unbelievable in your commitment to one another. You show us all a new definition of love. May God continue to bless you as you continue to bless one another and us. (Bonni)

*   *   *

It's not a revelation to say that because one's body is all connected, having a misaligned jaw means issues in my neck, shoulders, back, hips and even feet. These are the areas my physiotherapist has been addressing. So far he has not touched my jaw.

My physiotherapist is an Egyptian Christian who immigrated to Canada at age 35, now 24 years ago. He wanted to spare his children "what he experienced" and give his family a better life. He also desired to continue learning and growing professionally, something denied in Egypt because of his faith.

Rafaat is a gentle, soft-spoken and respectful man. From my initial meeting he insisted that I tell him if anything hurt or if I was simply nervous about the treatment. If so, he would stop. He's also highly skilled. Routinely declares, "This spot hurts," before he has touched what seems to be a random place on my neck or back and I almost always concur. "Yes, that is tender," to which he replies, "Thank you," and promptly makes it better.

Yesterday, my fifth session, he asked a new question. "I would like to work on your jaw now. Is that okay with you?"

My mind and heart raced. "What will you be doing?" I dared inquire. He explained about deep bone bruising and how the technique he used would aid in the healing process, assuring me several times that he would quit at any point if I became uncomfortable. I said yes.

Logically speaking, letting Rafaat hold my chin and apply pressure centimetres from where my bone now ends and becomes metal makes no sense. Why on earth would I risk anything going sideways when I've had such an incredible recovery?

Later in the day, I recalled my teaching life and how I used a formula to illustrate a point to the class. It went like this: T = CB / T (Read: T equals CB over T). I would allow participants a few minutes to try to solve the problem and then we'd discuss how Trust develops when we see Consistent Behavior over Time in a person. I let Rafaat work on my jaw because he has earned my respect and proven himself trustworthy over the short time I've known him.

When he finished the treatment he asked, "How does that feel? It should feel lighter." In that moment, with elastic bands on my teeth limiting my opening, all I could return was that it hadn't hurt. And really, what does a lighter jaw feel like anyway? He smiled, and I left, pleased that "first" was now behind me.

When I ate dinner last night, with my bands removed, it took a few bites to register. "Bill, my jaw feels more natural." We must have been quite the sight as I repeatedly opened and closed my mouth, feeling less tension in the joints. He cheered as I tried to find words for it feeling "more like my own, less mechanical, more fluid."

Every day I learn more about trust in practical terms and the faith it requires to take risks, big or small. That struck me afresh when we looked at the surgeon's blueprints and saw a warning from the makers of the prosthetic joints. "Caution: Last screw is less than 2 mm from brain cavity."

While I am choosing to trust these skilled people who are assisting me toward a new jaw life, ultimately, my trust is in the Lord. He knows even the number of hairs on my head, which, incidentally, are growing back. He is trustworthy.

I'm not sure if it's related to yesterday's treatment or not but another first occurred early this morning. Bill greeted me with, "Good morning, you look thinner. Your face looks thinner." Music to my less chubby ears.

* * *

Perhaps we got a little cocky. Or maybe it's just one of those times when a well-measured, weighed and thought-out plan isn't such a good idea after all.

Anyone we've asked around here about ideas for short outings recommends St. Jacobs, an area about an hour from us that boasts a year-round farmer's market with hundreds of vendors where local growers and Old Order Mennonite farmers sell their produce and wares. The market is open three days a week—Tuesday, Thursday and Saturday, with Tuesday being the smallest, least busy version. We chose Tuesday.

The skies were overcast and provided a welcomed canopy for the open space of the market. The cloud also introduced us to one of Ontario's signature features—humidity. By simply opening the car door we knew we had entered a different phase of our stay here.

The market lived up to its billing and provided us with fresh produce and baked treats at wonderful prices. We tried the famous apple fritters and Bill found some new sunglasses for the upcoming sockeye season. Our time was pleasant and I navigated through my first Maxilla-on-the-road session successfully. Yes, she works in the front seat of a car, too.

Such a pleasant day. Until. About five minutes before our departure, I noticed the sky becoming charcoal gray. Within minutes, the deluge began and we started our drive home with lightning flashes, thunder claps, road construction and soon after, rush hour traffic.

Traffic on the 401 has a crazy high percentage of semi-trucks, likely due, at least in part, to the logistics role Mississauga plays in our country. Take a peek at your cereal box. There's a good chance your Cheerios were packaged here. And all those big trucks in heavy traffic with pouring rain at the end of a lovely but full first real outing day—you get the picture. I was beyond spent by the time we arrived home.

In many ways my recovery is deceptive. I am making great strides and looking less and less like a surgical patient each day. But the fact is, just four weeks ago today I underwent major, eight-hour surgery. Perhaps when they told me to plan on a full year of recovery they weren't kidding.

So, we live and learn. In the future, I think we'll make a reasonable plan, given what we think I can handle, and then cut it in half, leaving margin for life's unexpected storms. I knew recovery would be up and down, trial and error, pushing and backing off, and yesterday was all of the above. Thankfully, no harm was done in any major sense, but I am certainly weary. Back to resting.

*   *   *

Four times a day I position myself in front of the mirror, look myself directly in the eyes, take a breath, make sure my shoulders are relaxed, and then stretch. In addition to Maxilla sessions, I use the same location to wind elastics around my braces using tweezers to reach the far back teeth and also to painstakingly clean and then apply vitamin E to scars on my temples and neck. In short, I look at my own face a great deal these days.

Imagine my surprise when, a couple of days ago, I realized that my ears had relocated.

Surprisingly, Chris Hadfield's memoir, *An Astronaut's Guide to Life on Earth: What Going to Space Taught Me About Ingenuity, Determination, and Being Prepared for Anything* is shedding light on my ear situation. I love how God brings certain books across my path at key times and how an author puts words to my experience, simply by writing theirs. This is proving to be one such book.

His story intrigues me generally but my curiosity piqued with the chapter titled "The Power of Negative Thinking." For years I encouraged people to look at the role attitude plays in career. Consequently, I began reading with anticipation of a "bad attitudes are bad for you" perspective. Not so.

In fact, one of Hadfield's premises is that negative thinking—considering the worst possible case scenario, and then preparing for it—is key to his success as an astronaut. I was hooked as he described the array of simulations he participated in with NASA attempting to address every eventuality. In the end he concludes that going through all these disastrous possibilities did not leave him depressed, but rather, prepared.

To some degree, I can relate. The news back in November that I required major surgery with high risk caused me to consider possibilities. I swirled around in "what if's" and "oh no's" for a while and had many conversations with the Lord about it. I also processed the risks—even the possibility of dying—with a few key people brave enough to tackle the topic with me.

In retrospect I see that God directed me in ways not unlike the astronaut's preparation. I'd ask myself, "If I do die or am severely incapacitated, what can I do today that would make things easier for those I love?" That question led to practical, purposeful activity and turned my attention away from fretting and toward action. I wrote letters, put a list of my passwords (at least the ones I can remember) in our safety deposit box, initiated important conversations—in short, I put my affairs in order.

Some letters were sent, while others, like this one to my husband and sons, were not, but they helped me surrender the outcomes to the Lord and were left behind, just in case.

I wrote:

What I'd like you to know...

Mostly, I want you to know that I love you—always have, always will—no matter what happens.

Just in case...

I wrestle almost daily with whether or not to write these letters. Part of me stands firmly in faith that God has clearly directed me into this surgery and that He will protect and bring me through it. However, just as quickly, I step back and reflect on how often God's ways are mysterious and A + B does not always = C. I want to believe that a successful outcome and a full, healthy recovery would give God glory and accomplish His purposes just fine. I am no longer so naïve.

So from the place of letting go of the outcome and leaning hard on belief that God is good, no matter what, I write to you. Just in case…

Just in case something goes drastically awry during the operation and I don't survive it, I hope you will remember that God is still good. When I think of this being a possible ending place of my life, I know that death is not what brings sorrow. I will be fine. What I grieve is the sorrow you will feel and the ways such a loss threatens to unsettle and challenge one's faith and outlook. I believe that you are well equipped to find your way along and pray that, in the midst, you will press hard toward God with your questions, anger, fears, sadness or whatever else the experience is for you. Surround yourself with people who love God and love you and are willing to do the raw work of grief.

Just in case…do know that I will miss participating with you in the momentous and most ordinary moments of your future. The obvious voids come to mind of celebrations and adventures but mostly I feel sad at the thought of not having tea with you, not hearing about the experiences of living daily, not sharing deck time or fireplace chats. Those losses I grieve most.

I have every confidence that you will live well and I also know enough about life to know that you will sustain blows. God is still good and for you. Our world is broken and sinful and this side of heaven, there will be crap. Nothing that happens here changes who God is and how much He loves you.

Of course there is a great likelihood that I will make it through surgery. Just in case there are complications, know that I will do everything within my realm to become well and strong and able to enter life again. And where there are deficits and things I simply can't change or work harder to heal or fix, I ask for grace and patience. My heart is to run with you and climb mountains and jump from rock to rock and hold the little hands of grandchildren and tell stories and be the kind of mom and grandma you want to hang out with. I will try to find my way to that place. By God's grace, I will try.

Much love,

Shelaine/Mom

Hadfield is right. It didn't depress me to think and act in these "worst case scenario" ways, it actually empowered me and reduced anxiety. So when the day came to walk down the hall to the operating theatre, I felt prepared, even a little excited and aware that hundreds of people were praying for God's peace upon me.

But back to my ears. I'm reminded of Bill and me sitting, pre-surgery, with a six-page document, each sheet full of risks and each statement requiring my initials. I read and gave consent, 35 times over, acknowledging that I was informed of all the possible bad-news scenarios they could think of. I don't recall them mentioning the relocation of ears.

And the moral of the story for me is, as prepared as I try to be, there will always be surprises and unexpected twists. That's where my posture, literally, of opening my hands and lifting my palms to the Lord, reminds me to let go of the outcome. I can do my planning and preparation, and should in many cases, but ultimately I choose to have faith in God for His best.

So, about my ears. It's not like they are on upside down or backwards. They simply aren't where they used to be and it wasn't until the swelling around them decreased significantly that it even registered. They used to sit flat on my head and were more upright. Now, due to skin stretching, I imagine, they have a slightly reclined look and peek out from my scalp a little. Bill says he hadn't noticed and once my thick locks return, others won't likely either—except for those who read this.

I choose to see my reconfigured ears as a reminder to thank God that my hearing is unaffected, I have no facial paralysis, fallen brows, drooping eyelids, infection, or numb cheeks—a few of the possibilities on the consent form I signed.

*   *   *

"Do you want me to add anything to Shelaine's homework? Anything in addition to her neck mobilization exercises?" Kelly, the kineseologist at the physiotherapy clinic, asked Rafaat.

"Yes, start her on some core strengthening," he replied.

Oh no. Hold on right there. I signed up for the jaw rehabilitation program. Let's leave my soggy abdomen out of this deal, I thought. But instead of protesting, I complied (because of that trust thing, although this felt more like the "obey" factor) and climbed onto the treatment table.

"Okay, lie flat, bend your knees and put two fingers just on the inside of each pelvic bone," she instructed. So far so good.

"Now pull your muscles down to the bed and swoop them up toward your navel."

"Pardon me? You want me to do what?" I asked, not really trying to stall but also not minding delaying the inevitable. She patiently explained the concept again, three times, using a different word picture each time.

"Okay, give it a try. Tighten up those core muscles."

I did try. Honestly. And then asked sincerely, "What muscles?" She seemed to think I was joking. I tried again.

"No, relax your shoulders. Stop holding your breath. Push your pelvis into the table. Don't tighten your diaphragm." So many directives, so little success! My spirits rose, however, when she told me how having three babies effectively obliterates core muscles. *Yes, I've been exonerated from these dreadful drills* ran through my head when I heard, "Okay, five more please!"

I have to confess, as crazy as this may sound, I'd rather do the work of Maxilla.

Maxilla and I have an understanding. She does her part, I do mine and together we are producing beautiful, tangible, visible results, albeit through an extremely painful process. The pain factor is certainly much lower with these abdominal workouts, largely because muscles you can't find don't hurt much. But it's greater than that, and once again, feels like a metaphor for my journey.

Core strengthening reminds me of the two years I spent off work and waiting for surgery. When Kelly first asked me to do this exercise I felt lost within my own body. This was new ground and I was floundering to find something familiar. I couldn't do it on my own. It was only when Kelly said, "Okay, off the table. Here. Put your fingers on my abdomen and feel what my muscles are doing," that I started to get the picture.

Similarly, during those early months of medical leave, as I read books like *Being Well When We're Ill* and *When the Heart Waits,* I caught glimpses of how periods of waiting looked in the lives of others. I intentionally observed people in difficult circumstances to glean how to live well. In short, I couldn't do it alone. I needed, and continue to need, outside input and accountability to strengthen my core.

There's nothing glamorous about doing core strengthening. You lie on your back and do these tiny incremental movements so slight that anyone observing might think you are cloud watching. And so it was in those waiting years. I had to learn to value the smallest accomplishments and come to terms with simply being.

Core strengthening takes time. It's an investment in a solitary activity that shows little reward for a long time and feels very unsatisfying at times. Throughout the two years prior to surgery, I had a soul-level confidence that I was exactly where God wanted me to be and that waiting and taking care of myself—in all senses of the term—was my vocation. And yet, at times, it felt akin to crawling a marathon. Many days I felt like I did on that physio table asking God, "What muscles?" or, "How do you want me to live today?"

Core strengthening is actually ridiculously hard work. Now that the muscles are engaged and actively tightening, I know exactly where they are! And I have this sneaking suspicion that I won't get a graduation certificate from core work on July 14th. I'd love a little ceremony where Kelly says, "Well done,

Shelaine, you've finally figured out how to do this. Be free to live your life now."

Ha! I already know that's not going to be the talk I get. It's more likely to be, "Core strengthening is the foundation to the structural wellbeing of your whole body. Do these exercises until you get to heaven and you'll be able to move on to strengthen other parts of your body and avoid injury." I just know it.

But what I also know is this: the core strengthening program God took me on for two intense years prepared me for this challenge. Every day I see another way that the prelude readied me for the big show. I suspect now that losses, sacrifices, choices to trust God in everyday matters were all part of God's workout regime, intended to build up my muscles of perseverance and contentment. The hard work has been worth it.

* * *

"Happy Anniversary!" It's been one month since surgery —a month of euphoric recognition that my pre-operation pain is gone. Perhaps I am most astounded at the absence of agony when I observe the gouging tool marks on my old plates illustrating the surgeon's difficulty removing them. How intense my pain must have been when I consider that bones being cut off, twenty-four magenta screws drilled into my skull and chin and four large incisions don't touch those previous levels. There is nothing to do but give thanks to God for His mercy and provision of such a skilled surgeon and reflect on what has become our theme: "Now to Him who is able to do immeasurably more than all we ask or imagine, according to

His power that is at work within us, to Him be glory in the church and in Christ Jesus, throughout all generations, forever and ever." (Ephesians 3:20-21)

One month ago. Kind of feels like three years.

*   *   *

Exiting the front doors yesterday morning reminded us of our time in Indonesia where the humidity hangs thick in the air and leaves you dripping after taking a few steps. It was a sticky walk to church.

Last week we took the same eight minute walk to the Cineplex movie complex and attended the African Methodist church, in Theatre Ten, where we enjoyed half an hour of delightful, energetic, meaningful and loud singing before I needed to leave. On our departure, we noticed another church beginning at 10:30 a.m. and that's where we decided to go yesterday.

We arrived at Cineplex about 10:25, walked past the closed popcorn and candy concession, and proceeded to Theatre 3, our destination church. It felt a bit odd to not be welcomed by anyone, usher or ticket taker, but we carried on up the walkway. Empty. The church had vanished.

We suspect we missed the memo of a church picnic or something but that didn't help us in the moment. What to do? We did know the church in Theatre Ten would be finished most of the beautiful, boisterous, exhausting singing. And the start time last week did seem quite fluid. So back we went.

The usher welcomed us and showed us to seats as the worship team of twelve led "Great is Thy Faithfulness." Three songs later we were seated and the service moved on. Around 11:30 the senior pastor took the microphone. Bill asked, "Can you stay for the sermon?"

"Yes, I think I can." We sat back in our comfy chairs.

But it wasn't the sermon. The senior pastor, who we later discovered is Brian Warren, a former CFL all-pro linebacker, popular motivational speaker and recently appointed co-host of the 700 Club TV show, started sharing prayer requests and answers to prayer. His highly articulate, rapid-fire delivery and regular calls for congregational response kept us challenged to follow. At one point I turned to Bill and whispered, "Is he talking about Trinity?" He nodded, "I think so."

We were so encouraged to find out this congregation has been fervently praying for Trinity Western University. I thought for a minute Bill might stand up and shout, "Hey, I teach there," which would likely have been fine in this free-flowing service. In fact, we both wished after that he had!

At noon I leaned over and let Bill know I was fading, and the sermon had yet to begin. The offering presented a natural point to sneak out as people streamed down to the front to give their gifts. Just for the record, you don't sneak in or out of this church! Solomon, an usher, intercepted us, gathered another member and the two of them prayed for us and for my healing in particular. They also signed us up for the church BBQ, men's Bible study, outdoor baptism service...I don't think they quite caught that we are leaving the province in two weeks.

Not to worry though, Bill went to the corner store later in the day and bumped into Solomon, who was just returning home from church...at 2:30! Bill clarified our situation and later Bill and I decided that if we go back next week, we'll pack a lunch. I actually had wondered why so many people around us were eating sandwiches during announcement time.

Overall, we felt like we were exactly where God wanted us to be yesterday morning. Sometimes that direction is clearer than others, like when the church you plan to attend disappears.

* * *

Today is moving day and we are mostly ready to go. At first changing units felt like a minor inconvenience and then we got excited about living on the other side of the building, not to mention our gratitude that we actually have a place to reside in this same building. But just in case there remained any negative feelings about leaving the 32nd floor...we had another fire alarm at 5:00 yesterday afternoon and got to walk 448 stairs down again. Our calves say "enough" and we rejoice in being 308 steps closer to the ground.

When I first learned we would need to change condos I felt much like I did when the nurse said, "Okay, you need to get up and start walking." Both just seemed like bad ideas. The possibility of blood clots and a further weakened constitution got me out of bed in the hospital and the idea of sharing our condo with strangers convinced me to move.

It's just that staying the same often feels easier and more comfortable than changing.

However, we've come to see the move as symbolic. We appreciated the bubble effect the stratosphere of our 32nd floor provided during the acute phase of recovery. It seems that people who live up so high are quiet folk, perhaps due to the thinner air. We rarely saw anyone, heard anything and felt like we were free to fully focus on recovery and wellbeing.

I could look down from the lofty vantage point of our balcony, watch commotion in City Square and feel connected to human activity without being in it. The vista across downtown Mississauga was wide open, and spectacular sunsets provided natural beauty in the midst of urban living.

Now we live on the 10th floor on the opposite side of the building in a one-bedroom unit. There are far more people around and the balconies are close enough that we could actually get to know our neighbors. The courtyard below is beautifully kept and I can differentiate hostas from lilac bushes instead of things simply looking like green space.

In these weeks I don't need the security and isolation of being "high up" but rather need the exercise and outings that build strength without much talking. We may even choose to take the stairs rather than wait for the elevators.

I feel like I'm being gradually lowered into life again.

Our new view straight out is largely dominated by another condo building which prevents us from seeing a panorama of the area. If we look only in that direction the sights are simply brick and mortar. But if we shift our eyes to the right we see trees and houses and to the left, lake, and Toronto in the distance. Looking up we take in puffy white clouds backed by blue skies and eyes down reveal manicured gardens. The view seems to have a lot to do with where I choose to gaze.

And I choose to look forward, filled with hope and excitement for what lies ahead. Part of our new outlook includes a tennis court and this morning I said to Bill, "I'm going to play tennis again," to which he replied, "I know you will." I'm so thankful he believes in me.

And I choose to look back, intentionally reflecting on God's goodness and remembering His provisions, healing and mercy. It's easy to forget and take for granted. This morning I was three quarters of the way through my piece of toast when I realized it hadn't taken any effort or attention to bite, chew and swallow it, something unheard of one short month ago.

Today we'll sit on our balcony knowing that the people of Mississauga are descending on City Square to celebrate Canada Day and we won't be able to see it all. But that's okay because now we can go join them, if we want to. Perhaps we'll even have another Beaver Tail.

* * *

Biting into a whole fresh nectarine is exhilarating. Yawning without bracing for pain is invigorating. Chewing chunks of chicken with ease is exciting. Sneezing without gasping is a relief. Crunching on a dill pickle chip is thrilling. But none of those come close to what I experienced yesterday for the first time in far too long.

Back when the news of my need for surgery broke, a group of close friends decided that they wanted to fundraise and cover the costs we would incur—roughly $22,000. That's the portion our medical plan doesn't cover because the jaw is considered a dental issue, plus all the costs of living in Ontario for two months. BC medical did pay for the prosthetic joints—another $20,000—and most of my hospital stay. We were and remain incredibly grateful for the vision and efforts of friends who have taken financial stress out of this journey.

Early in the process, Wendy, the leader of the fundraising group, told me who was on the committee and that they had met, but graciously kept me quite out of the loop. I had no idea what they were planning and somehow that felt easier. It's humbling to be the recipient of such extravagant work and generosity.

One morning months ago I sent Wendy an email and said, "I had a hilarious dream last night. It was about a comedy improv night called Medical Maladies." Her reply, "Hmm, that's interesting. We're looking into having Panic Squad and your boys do an improv show as a fundraiser!" Hmm, indeed!

Fast forward two months and many details coming together in miraculous ways and the show took place. It was particularly meaningful to have all three of our sons involved in the hilarious antics and to have my parents join us from Manitoba, and my sister and her family be there as well. The night was encouraging, zany and jump-started a generous flow of donations. And, it was full of jaw-busting laughter.

As much as my family and I love the funny side of life, laughter has been one of my greatest sources of pain and surely one of my greatest felt losses. For over three years I've restrained myself, refrained from yukking it up and generally needed to take a far too serious posture many times. And when I didn't, I paid a high pain price.

Yesterday morning Bill and I went on a long walk and on our return trip we encountered a particularly spectacular flowerbed with an intriguing plant I've never seen before. We stopped so I could take a picture with my phone and Bill jumped in the shot. I kept moving and he kept shifting positions and between bright sun shining from behind and me not wearing my glasses. . .we lost it and ended up in doubled-over, heavy duty, cracking-up-so-onlookers-wonder-about-your-wellbeing laughter.

I laughed without pain! It didn't hurt during and it didn't hurt after. In fact, it wasn't until we got home and I found myself chuckling over the incident that it registered. I laughed freely and hard and suffered no consequences! That may be the single biggest gift I receive with this new jaw. "Our mouths were filled with laughter, our tongues with songs of joy. Then it was said among the nations, 'The Lord has done great things for them.'" (Psalm 126:2)

* * *

In addition to laughter, there have been tears, but surprisingly few. In fact, Bill recounts to friends the first time I've cried since surgery.

July 2, 2014

For all the good we have experienced from the start of this ordeal three years ago (or thirty-five), we have also known hard times and challenges that will leave indelible marks on us. One thing of course is Shelaine's new scars.

For those of you who know Shelaine up close and personal, you might wonder how you missed her first set of scars from her 1980 surgery. I remember her pointing them out to me on one of our early dates, pulling back her hair by her ears to show the top ones and tilting her jaw to point to the under ones. Both had long faded and blended into the contours of her jaw and natural crease lines.

When we talked about incisions with Dr. Psutka, he said he would follow the old scars near her ears. Not so with the neck ones. And fair enough. Shelaine's 1980 surgeon used the jaw line incision only to pull her jaw downward so he could remove the cartilage. But her recent surgery required room to saw off jawbone and screw on metal mandibles. Dr. Psutka couldn't simply follow the old 1.5 inch scars under her chin.

When we were at church last week and two leaders prayed with us, I explained that Shelaine had just had surgery on her jaw. Shelaine turned her head so Gavin and Solomon could see her scars. Gavin replied, "Oh. I hadn't noticed." And that seems to be the case with others as well.

Yesterday, when I reminded Shelaine that I wanted to write this post, I made a joke about the scars that I now fully regret. (Sometimes my impetuous self overrides my redeemed self.) That led to tears, several apologies, and a good conversation about how I see her now, scars and all.

I had to admit that when the bandages first came off I saw her scars as unsightly crooked lines marring her pretty face. Add the swelling, and one couldn't help but say she looked different. But as you have seen, with pictures posted, and from the testimony of Sue and Wendy, Shelaine's swollen features have diminished and her scars melded. And they will continue to fade.

After telling Shelaine how I saw things back then, I told her how I am coming to see them now. Scars may be skin deep, but they tell a story that is heart-deep.

To me Shelaine's scars tell the story of her making a difficult choice that led to increased pain, for long-term gain, and that signals courage.

To me they tell the story of her spiritual journey from way back, making meaning of chronic pain and helping others suffering from similar ailments. I have learned so much watching her along this path.

To me they tell the story of love for any future little people she hopes to hold firmly in strong arms, and smiling while up-stretched tiny hands stroke her face and ask, as children do, "What's that?" I imagine her saying, "Let me tell you the story about those scars..."

To me Shelaine's scars are the narrative of a determined woman who has refused to roll over and let life do her in; she has received this challenge as a gift from which to re-shape her identity, learn new skills, and become a more intriguing person. I am so fortunate to be married to her and to be her best friend.

And she's beautiful to me. And I told her so.

* * *

It's July the Fourth, Independence Day in America and cause for me to reflect on that quality within. Independence is, by definition:

1. The state or quality of being independent.

2. Freedom from the control, influence, support, aid, or the like, of others.

It's possible my family members would tell you I was born with an independent spirit. They would share stories about the day, as a 4 or 5 year old, that I darted between the closing doors of an elevator in Eaton's department store, leaving my mother and grandmother behind. I couldn't understand all the fuss when they found me. I was *fine*. In fact, it had been a rather exhilarating ride!

I also recall my grandmother telling me, just before I left for university, that she thought the song *I Did It My Way* was written for me.

Let's face it, I was an only child for my first five years and then moved into the first-born role where I took on some over-achieving, perfectionist qualities. So whether it's nature or nurture or combination, the net effect is an independent spirit that has, admittedly, served me well in many areas of life.

But just to state the obvious: not always.

Dependence:

1. The state of relying on or needing someone or something for aid, support, or the like.

2. Reliance; confidence; trust:

Before we left Abbotsford, Bill and I had a conflict rooted in my concern over whether or not he would advocate for me while I was incapacitated. I'd resolved the possibility of dying but it felt unnerving to think I could be totally dependent on him and others for my care, safety and wellbeing.

The potential for being in need of someone to do everything for me, for an extended period of time, was real. I had one specialist (not Dr. Psutka) tell me, when speaking of this very surgery, that when I woke up from it I would wish I had died on the table. Great marketing! But even the voices I trusted prepared me for an excruciating, gruelling, long haul. My circumstances were about to require that I rely on or need "someone or something for aid, support, or the like."

It was then that I realized I had another choice to make.

A few years ago, Bill trapped a possum in our backyard. It had been tearing up freshly laid sod and seemed to be moving in under our shed. Bill built a homemade contraption he dubbed the *Possum 2000* and placed the bait. Several days later we awoke to the animal equivalent of a swearing outrage. The caged critter was spitting mad about his newly imposed circumstances and would not have smiled and raised a paw of thanks if Bill had offered to feed and care for him. (Just for the record, Bill relocated him to a rural park...carefully.)

That possum became dependent on Bill, due to its caged condition, and he fought tooth and nail all the way to his freedom. While I was willingly walking into my "caged" equivalent, I realized before I entered the hospital that I got to choose, in many respects, what kind of patient I would be. Would I fight for independence and stubbornly try to do things on my own? Or, would I surrender my will and accept, with gratitude, the care being offered?

Thankfully, by God's grace, I believe I've been able to do more of the latter. I haven't driven a car in over seven weeks nor have I carried a purse. I required personal shoppers to locate a gala dress and couldn't think clearly enough to figure out medications for the first while. I haven't made a meal (okay, so that one isn't too hard to accept!) in weeks and the bathroom is pretty much the only place where I am alone (and not even there in those first days!). My ability to relax into the recovering role has been made easier because the one I've depended on has been gracious, reliable and trustworthy.

Yesterday, I walked—alone—to Starbucks from the spot on the lake where Bill was fishing. It felt good, but not from a caged, "I need out" sense. Rather, it felt like a natural progression of healing.

Perhaps it really comes down to God answering the request of one of my most faithful prayer warriors, 3-year-old Ben Petker. Ben routinely asks God to "help Mrs. Strom not scream and to be a good girl."

* * *

I do laundry.

I have been dependent on Bill to do almost everything, but even in the earlier weeks of recovery, Bill would wash and dry clothes and then bring the basket to me for folding. I learned years ago that it's important to contribute, even in small ways, as I can.

We have friends, Kevin and Allyson Martin and their kids, who have been missionaries in Indonesia for almost 25 years. Many times during their return to Canada, the Martins have used our home as a landing pad and place to get over jet lag. On one occasion we even made T-shirts sporting Kibbutz '97 to commemorate our 5-week merging of families, including six preschoolers under our roof!

These were meaningful times for us as we renewed friendship, got to know each other's children well and built new relationships with Kevin and Allyson's extended family. Enter Dave and Margy Martin.

I vividly recall a season when the Martin seniors would come to visit and Margy would struggle to make it up our seven front stairs. She was in a waiting season for hip replacements. But what I recall even more poignantly is how she would find her way to the couch and say, "Please bring me the laundry. I'll fold." Keep in mind with six kids and six adults in the house, this was a never-ending task!

And she didn't just fold. She did it with joy, delightful conversation and no complaint. And when it was time to prepare supper, she would make her way to the kitchen table, take up a knife and chop vegetables with the same spirit. Not only did I appreciate her help, I admired her character and approach to life.

In her book, *Better Than My Dreams*, Paula Rinehart says, "People who have let go of their expectations of how they think life is supposed to look usually stumble upon gratitude —which is a wonderful thing to find. You stop waiting for life to begin when it's fixed and all the broken parts are healed. It's now, in *this* moment, *this* conversation, *this* sunset."

I suspect Margy didn't expect to find herself sidelined from the mission field of Indonesia, awaiting surgery. And yet she embraced her situation and found joy in the midst. In our home, I watched as she engaged in conversations with kids flying through the living room and I benefited greatly from her example and words of encouragement.

If you were to ask Margy about this, I think she'd be quick to say that she was able to live as she did because of Christ who gives her strength. She'd likely also point out that God taught her "the secret of being content in any and every situation, whether well fed or hungry, whether living in plenty or in want." (Phil 4:12b)

I also know that she made choices to give thanks in all circumstances, even when folding laundry.

And that's why, as I keep growing up, I want to be like Margy.

*   *   *

I can read again now that I'm not fidgeting and changing positions every three minutes due to pain. The arm-less pince-nez glasses Bill crafted for me perch on the end of my nose and I dive back into Canadian astronaut Chris Hadfield's book.

Hadfield says, "You have to try, consciously, to help others succeed. Some people feel this is like shooting themselves in the foot—why aid someone else in creating a competitive advantage? I don't look at it that way. Helping someone else look good doesn't make me look worse. In fact, it often improves my own performance, particularly in stressful situations."

This quote brought to mind the philosophy of my first boss at Strategic, Lindsay Brooks. I distinctly recall him saying to me on more than one occasion that his goal was to give people work opportunities where they could become better than him at something. He saw his company as a training ground for people to learn, grow and then move into whatever else God called them to, taking their newly-gained skills and experience with them.

His philosophy made sense to me and I bought in.

Particularly in my later years at Strategic, I intentionally looked for ways to build into my co-workers by encouraging them to take further education, giving opportunities to try out teaching and mentoring them in working with clients. And Hadfield is right. Their success didn't make me look worse; in fact, it held me accountable to grow professionally and pushed me to be better at my craft. It was a win/win. And it didn't feel like work because it was fun. I loved it!

Wouldn't that be a nice place to end this story?

The truth is, helping others succeed was not much of a sacrifice when my own career flourished. But when I moved into a season of medical leave, my philosophy became harder work. I recall my trusted counsellor empathizing and saying, "Shelaine, you're at a stage of life when many women spread their wings and fly. Your wings have been clipped." I appreciated his validation of the challenge but I still had some wrestling to do.

Some parts of this journey are just painful. Each time I said no to a great offer to speak or passed a contract onto a co-worker or watched someone I had coached sail on to amazing new opportunities it took me some time to process all the emotion it stirred. I felt disappointed for myself yet excited for my friends. I felt relief that I didn't have to work and continue pushing through ridiculous pain to earn a paycheck. I felt grief over lost chances, people not met, and challenges not overcome. In short, at times I felt like a mess.

It's that very mess, and a willingness to sit in it, that drove me back to the basics again and again. Do I believe that God is good? Do I believe that I am loved and not forgotten? Do I believe that God's best is and will always be for my best? Yes, yes and yes. So I chose to trust and wait.

From this vantage point, it looks a little different now. I observe that I never did die of disappointment and I've been blessed beyond words to see how friends have grown and blossomed. Medical leave has afforded me rest at a core level that I didn't even know I needed and time to build into important relationships. But most significantly, I'm seeing that God has taken this season, that I offered up to Him, and breathed life into it in ways I never in a million years could have seen coming.

Perhaps this topic surfaces because I feel our focus shifting here. We're looking in the freezer and having conversations about what we'd better eat soon. We're buying thank you cards for the physio team and making arrangements for getting to the airport.

I know that when I get home, I have many more months to spend cheering my people on from the sidelines. There will be times when it's hard, I know from experience, but that's okay. I have much to be grateful for and, in the depths of my soul, I know that He who began a good work will be faithful to complete it.

Epilogue

I celebrated my three year surgical anniversary with over 350 hours of rehabilitation, a dozen massage therapy treatments, forty-eight physiotherapy appointments, and 95,000+ Maxilla stretches behind me. It's been quite the journey.

The road of healing post-surgery has been arduous, and God and I have worked diligently to get to this place. My physiotherapist routinely calls me "a machine" as I confidently squat down and up again with ease. He says he hardly recognizes me. It makes me smile to be the strongest and most physically fit that I've been since I was a teen athlete.

Many goals, some intentionally set and others stumbled upon, have been met in this season. Writing kept me sane and resulted in my first book called, *Changing Course: Stories to Navigate Career and Life Transitions,* published in October 2016. God used the experience of capturing previous work stories to bring closure to my own job loss and benefit others going through career and work transitions.

In December of 2015, I recognized both an emotional and physical preparedness to re-enter the work world. I had no job to return to. So I determined to establish a private consulting business. But in what? I loved my past life as a career and life coach so that seemed a natural fit. However, leading training workshops and facilitating groups previously energized me. And public speaking…that's just fun!

And what about this new-found passion for writing? Had it simply provided a means to sanity during my "ministry of obscurity" years, or did God desire me to carry on with it?

Fairly quickly I began to feel like a jack-of-all-trades and master of none. I know that marketing gurus say to find your niche market and run with it, but committing to only one area created inner distress over letting go of the others.

Just prior to Christmas I attended a walk-through event at a local Christian retreat center. The evening focused on preparing our hearts for celebrating Jesus' birth and, at the end of the tour, it offered an opportunity for participants to meet with a prayer team.

I felt drawn—no, more like pulled—into the prayer experience. I introduced myself to the three people and then sat quietly as they individually asked God what He would like to say to me through them. All that followed stunned me.

In turn, each person spoke of a picture or message God had impressed on their minds of me being one with a variety of gifts and that I shouldn't squelch any one of them, but rather embrace and celebrate each one. The details they gave were specific. I went home and promptly created a website with three categories for services I offer—career and life coaching, training workshops and event speaking—and a blog called *In the Midst*, and launched it on January 1, 2016.

And nothing happened.

A month after the site went live, I sent out another email to all my contacts letting them know I was back in business. It worked and I had three organizations book training workshops. Not a lot, but a start.

And then came an email from my old boss introducing me to the president of Food for the Hungry Canada (FH), stating that he thought I could "help FH with some training."

Arrangements were made and in mid-February I sat down with the president, believing he needed a session for his staff on personality style or some other workshop topic I present on. About 20 minutes into the discussion it dawned on me that I was in a job interview. We weren't having a consulting chat but rather discussing a permanent, half-time position.

The president described FH's need: someone to train and coach facilitators, someone to lead workshops, someone for speaking engagements, someone to write curriculum! How could I say no?

Since April of 2016 I have thanked God regularly for this life-giving, purpose-filled job that has taken me to Cambodia and multiple cities across Canada. You may recall the ongoing theme during surgery times of recognizing God's provisions and care being abundant and far more than we could have ever hoped for or imagined. Nothing has changed in that regard.

And on a family note, ours continues to grow with our sons in various stages of relationships with lovely young women. In October of 2016 a precious baby boy entered the world and confirmed to me that risking surgery with hopes of playing with grandchildren someday was also a worthy goal. I can hold him, look at his sweet face and anticipate the day he touches my scars and asks, "Grandma, what are these?"

Well, Grayson, let me tell you the story...

Study Questions

Pain and Loss

1. "Exhausted and afraid, I grieved the loss of the life I once knew." (p. 132) Identify the things Shelaine lost during her jaw journey. Which ones do you relate to?

2. Shelaine writes about grieving the loss of her job and with it a part of her identity. What losses have you experienced that have shaken your identity?

3. Describe how you have grieved losses in your own life.

4. What steps might you take to grieve in healthy ways?

5. At times, Shelaine chose to see her situation in a humorous light. In what ways can you bring levity to yours?

Pain and Waiting

1. What progression of thoughts and feelings do you see in Shelaine's article, *Waiting, The Passionate Pause*, (p.130)? What parts of this pattern may apply to your life?

2. During the waiting years, Shelaine describes feeling like broken pottery. (p. 63) How have you seen your life or identity as broken pottery, and how might Shelaine's story provide hope that God can bring the pieces together?

3. Consider and describe a time when the Potter has healed brokenness in your world. Try to name two or three specific provisions for which you are thankful.

4. Many examples in *But Pain Crept In* come from Shelaine's journals. What role did writing play in waiting? What role might journaling have in your story?

Pain and God's Sovereignty

1. On page 93, Shelaine asks, "If I truly believe that God is sovereign, then how does that change the way I live today? Practically speaking, where does the belief in a sovereign God intersect with my daily life?" What does the sovereignty of God mean to you? How would you answer Shelaine's ponderings?

2. In a letter to her sons, (p. 55), Shelaine says, "If there is anything I have learned on this health journey, it's that I see such a small portion of the picture. God's vision is perfect, mine so limited. I choose to trust Him." What does trusting God mean to you?

3. Shelaine showed gratitude in the midst of her difficult situation. How might a thankful spirit indicate her view of God's sovereignty?

4. What role does gratitude play amidst the challenges in your life?

Pain and Community

1. Shelaine says on page 129, "Being part of a community where people care is an incredible gift. I know that strangers and friends faithfully upheld me in prayer

and God used their acts of kindness on numerous occasions to encourage and sustain us through those wilderness years." What specific ways did their community support Shelaine and Bill?

2. Describe times of support and belonging you have experienced in the body of Christ? Have you experienced similar connection outside of the church?

3. If you haven't experienced this kind of community, what steps might you take to make this happen?

4. What kind of support do you need when you are struggling? What helps you feel understood?

5. What new ways of supporting distressed friends did you pick up from Shelaine's story?

Made in the USA
San Bernardino, CA
16 June 2018